Brandon's
Guide to Theater
in Asia

Brandon's
Guide to Theater
in Asia

JAMES R. BRANDON

The University Press of Hawaii
Honolulu

Unless otherwise noted photographs are by the author.

Library of Congress Cataloging in Publication Data

Brandon, James R
  Brandon's guide to theater in Asia.

  Includes bibliographies.
  1. Performing arts—Asia—Directories. I. Title.
II. Guide to theater in Asia.
PN2860.G8   1976   790.2'095   75–37506
ISBN 0–8248–0369–8

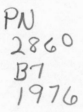

DEDICATION

To the hundreds of friends and theater people in Asia who have made theater-going such a pleasure for me over the years, I dedicate this book. My special thanks to Duane Hauch, Suresh Awasthi, Onoe Kuroemon, Roger Long, and Min-soo Ahn.

CONTENTS

Brandon's
Guide to Theater
in Asia

Introduction

Over the vast geographic area that is Asia, plays are performed in a thousand places—in luxuriously appointed modern theaters, in former royal palaces, in temple courtyards, and in temporary buildings made of bamboo and palm thatch. A rich feast of theater awaits the visitor, provided he, or she, knows where to go and what to expect. But it is not easy to discover where theaters are, what types of plays are being staged, or the hours, days, and seasons of performance. The purpose of this guide is to help the traveler in Asia find and enjoy exciting living theater.

First, a few hints about going to see theater in Asia. On the whole, playgoing is a more casual affair than it is in the West. Plays can last four or five hours. Some continue through the night until dawn. Starting times are not necessarily precise. People come and go during performance; you can too. Relax and enjoy yourself. Take the experience as it comes. Be ready to mingle with audiences from all levels of society (in contrast to Western audiences which today are mostly from the educated urban elite).

Be prepared to pick and choose from a truly immense range of theater. From India to Japan, the theater of Asia spreads out like a brilliant kaleidoscope. There are dance-dramas, ballets, masked pantomimes, operas, operettas, shadow-plays, doll-puppet plays, and more. From your place in the auditorium you will see not only actors and actresses, but elegant and exquisitely costumed court dancers, musicians, singers, chanters, and stage assistants. You will hear songs and heroic narratives and flights of poetic dialogue. Drums will thud and gongs will boom. Everywhere you go the colors, sights, and sounds will vary enormously from the last place. Since it is impossible for even the most fanatic theater buff to see everything, it is wise to know in advance the types of plays you are most interested in and to make your plans accordingly.

It is easy to find major theaters in Tokyo, Hong Kong, New Delhi, and a few other cities, but otherwise prepare to be on your own. You will have to hunt out even the best drama. When you arrive in a new city I suggest you do three things without fail.

First, buy a city map; carry it everywhere. Especially useful ones are mentioned by publisher's name in this guide, but any will do. With a map you can estimate distance, you can plot theater locations, you can plan a schedule that doesn't have you crisscrossing the city every day. With a map you can use local transportation. You can walk. Even if you intend to go everywhere by taxi, you will still find a map useful.

Second, spend an hour or so going over all English-language newspapers and magazines published in the city. No single publication will list all performances, but taken together they will give at least an idea of what is playing at major theaters. Read the papers daily. A notice may appear once only or there may be but a single performance. (If you can get your hotel clerk to translate for you, you will find more complete listings in vernacular papers.)

And third, ask, ask, and ask again. Most people you meet will not know what theaters are open. Or they may not understand your questions. Or they may not want a foreigner to go to a particular theater. There are a dozen reasons why your simple "where-can-I-see?" question can elicit a blank look or a negative reply. My own firm rule is: "Don't believe *no* until you've heard it three times." Hotel clerks may be helpful but don't depend upon it; they seldom have time for the unusual question, such as yours. I have good luck with taxi drivers. They almost always know where theaters are, once you can convince them you actually want to go to one and not to a movie. Or, phone or go to the national tourist bureau. The long and short of it is that except for a few major theaters everyone knows about you must play detective and you must never give up. After 25 years, I am still running across theaters that Asian friends have assured me do not exist.

There is no single Asia-wide theater season. Any time of the year will be good for theater somewhere. Urban theaters tend to be open year-round. Some will close in the hottest months of the year. In the countryside, some of Asia's most fascinating plays are performed only at religious festivals, or during specific seasons. The best time of year in tropical countries is the dry season (folk plays and dances simply halt during the torrential downpours of the rainy season). In the cool, dry fall and early winter months harvest and temple festival performances are seen throughout Asia's northern tier of countries, from India to Japan. Buddhist festival dates are reckoned by the lunar calendar, a month being 29 or 30 days. As a result, dates vary from year to year. If you haven't a moon-phase calendar (and who does?), watch for nights of the full moon, a common time for performances at Buddhist temples.

Buy the best seats in the house. I would never sit in the front row of a Broadway theater if I could avoid it, but in Asia I often do. You will find it fascinating to follow details of acting and dance, of costumes and makeup, of mask and puppet carving. And to do that you will want to be close. It's more comfortable up front, too; theaters are divided into first-, second-, third-, fourth-, and sometimes fifth-class sections; seats get narrower and harder as you move back from the stage. Tickets are very inexpensive—first class is seldom more than a dollar—so there is no reason not to treat yourself to a choice seat.

Should you buy tickets at the door or in advance? There is no simple answer to this question. Most of the time and in most places you can buy a ticket for a first-class seat at the door. You avoid hassle and aren't tied to a schedule this way. But some good performances may by SRO by curtain time. You may never have another chance. In a few countries you can make phone reservations. You may want to locate a theater during daylight hours, in which case you can buy your tickets at the same time. Tickets are conveniently sold at department stores and hotels in India, Singapore, and Japan (no agent's commission). It really depends on you—whether you like to plan carefully and have the assurance of tickets in hand or prefer to stay loose and uncommitted and take your chances. As a rule of thumb, I suggest: the fancier the theater and the more expensive the tickets, the wiser it is to buy or reserve in advance.

Now a bit about how to use this guide. Look up the country, or countries, you will be visiting. The fourteen countries described appear in alphabetical order. Only a few, important foreign terms are used; try to become familiar with them. Under **THEATERGOING** is general information on *THEATER BUILDINGS, THEATER SEASON, FESTIVALS, TRANSPORTATION,* and local sources of *INFORMATION.* "Program" means a printed program.

The section, **WHAT TO SEE**, briefly describes important dramatic forms of the country. Names of dramatic forms are in italic type (*Kabuki*). In no country in Asia are there fewer than three or four important forms; in India there are several dozen. Each is distinctive in its dance, musical, or dramatic style. Translating these names into English is impossible and in any case useless, for no one in Asia would understand the translation anyway. Learn these names as well as you can; you will have to use them. It's a good idea to ask your hotel clerk to write the name of a dramatic form in vernacular script to show a taxi driver if you have to hunt for a performance. To help you decide what you might want to see, one to four daggers (†) placed after the name of the dramatic form indicates its artistic value. To some extent this evaluation is personal, but as much as possible it reflects the way people of the country view their drama.

††††   Exceptional artistic value. Internationally recognized; superior performers; high-quality staging; dramatic or performance techniques of unusual interest, often (but not necessarily) old and traditional.

†††   High artistic value. Usually not well known outside its country; qualified professional performers; style of performance of considerable interest.

††   Moderate to slight artistic value. Professional or amateur performers of no particular reputation; may be popular entertainment; script, or performance, or staging lack substance.

†   Inferior artistic value. Extremely low performance and dramatic values; perhaps crude or vulgar; incompetent performers; poor staging.

You cannot go wrong with a four- or three-dagger dramatic form. The socially curious or the theater buff may find reason to seek out a one-dagger form. Two-dagger forms are often a bore.

Places where you can see plays are described in the section, **WHERE TO GO**. Urban theaters appear first; then towns and villages where special regional performances of importance occur on a regular, often annual, basis. Theaters within a city are listed alphabetically. A theater's name appears in in bold-face type (**Kabukiza**). Learn and use the vernacular name of a theater; rarely will an English translation of the name be known locally (the translation in parenthesis is for your convenience). A very few theaters are known only by English names. The quality of a theater and its convenience for foreign visitors is indicated by one to four stars. This rating is very largely a personal evaluation.

****   A first-class theater. Commonly frequented by foreign visitors; either of luxury quality or of special artistic significance; well-known; frequented by an elite audience; usually (but not always) new; excellent stage equipment; facilities such as restaurants; published programs; opera glasses for rent; air-conditioned and heated; comfortable seating.

***   A standard theater. Good audience facilities and stage equipment; air-conditioned and heated; comfortable, but not well-known to foreign visitors, and without special facilities for them.

** A minimal theater. Often a "hall" with a flat seating arrangement; lacks adequate stage equipment; audience facilities are basic; minimally comfortable and clean, but some inconvenience can be expected; rarely visited by foreign spectators and may be difficult to find.

* A below-standard theater. Perhaps freezing in winter and stifling in summer; often filthy; uncomfortable seating is likely; old building or temporary structure; hard to find and unknown; working-class or peasant audience.

As far as comfort and convenience go, you cannot miss with a four-star theater. Some are so beautiful that they are worth seeing regardless of what is playing. The insatiable, the adventurous, and perhaps the masochistic may be prepared to tolerate the discomfort of a one-star theater to savor its atmosphere and surroundings or to see a special play. There is no particular reason to seek out a two- or three-star theater for itself; if a good performance takes you there, fine. A two-dagger amateur modern play may be performed in a four-star luxury theater, and a four-dagger classical dance-drama may be seen in one- or two-star surroundings. The two separate rating systems are therefore used to help you choose not only what you want to see but where you want to see it.

At the end of each chapter (except for Hong Kong and Singapore) is a short reading list. The plays of Asia are both beautiful and complex. Your enjoyment of theater in Asia will be greatly enhanced if you spend some time reading up before starting your trip. You can buy books on theater in a few Asian countries, but finding what you want is extremely chancy.

At the back of this guide is a quick-reference Theater List, containing name, address, telephone number, hours of performance, ticket prices, and directions for finding each theater mentioned in the text. Prices are in local currency at the time of printing. Taxi fares are approximate and are calculated from the central train station or, if there is none, from the downtown area. Where noted, it is theater policy to have an English-speaking telephone operator or box-office person on duty; otherwise it's problematical whether English will be understood or not. You can try. Or ask your hotel operator to call for you.

Finally, remember that things change. New theaters are being built constantly; old ones may be torn down. Particularly subject to alteration are days a theater is open, type of performance, hours, and prices. Check regional performance dates when you arrive in a country; they may have changed. With the help of this guide you should be able to check, with relative ease, each theater you are interested in.

Happy theatergoing.

Books to Read

GENERAL: Faubion Bowers, *Theatre in the East* (New York: Grove Press, 1956); James R. Brandon, ed., *The Performing Arts in Asia* (Paris: UNESCO, 1971); A.C. Scott, *The Theatre in Asia* (New York: Macmillan, 1972).

PLAYS: G. L. Anderson, ed., *The Genius of the Oriental Theater* (New York: Mentor, 1966); James R. Brandon, ed., *Traditional Asian Plays* (New York: Hill and Wang, 1972); Vera Irwin, ed., *Four Classical Asian Plays* (Baltimore: Penguin, 1972).

Burma

A pristine country for the theatergoer to explore. Opened to tourists only a few years ago, Burma is not visited by many people. Masses of cars do not terrify pedestrians in Rangoon; Coca Cola and McDonald's are nowhere to be seen. Burma remains isolated and quiet, a self-contained, self-satisfied country. As Rangoon is a regular stop between Bangkok and New Delhi on international air routes, it is really quite easy to visit. Burmese theater has not attracted international attention. It is dynamic and amusing, but hardly deep or sophisticated. There are no real theater centers and, since there are no permanent theater buildings in Burma, looking for a performance can be a frustrating and, as often as not, futile affair. You are more likely to find performances in Rangoon and Mandalay than anywhere else.

In the past Burmese drama borrowed greatly from its neighbors—India on the west, China to the north, and Thailand on the east—but in style it is unique. Traditional plays bubble with mirth and gaiety. Theatrical dance is lively and carefree. Dance bursts out in brief spurts of breathtaking leaps, whirls, and kicks. The stage is a fairyland peopled by ravishingly handsome princes and vivacious princesses. Burmese clowns think nothing of taking an hour or two for their punning and pratfalls. The description of the Burmese as a happy and smiling person is borne out on the stage more than one would think possible. There are popular dance-plays, marionette plays, spirit-medium dances, and occasional performances of classical masked dances.

THEATERGOING

You will see the same types of plays performed throughout Burma. So, except for tribal dances found in remote hill areas, there is no need to travel into the hinterlands to seek out an important form of regional drama. Be prepared to hunt for any performances you go to, however. Language of performance is Burmese.

THEATER BUILDINGS. Burma is the only country in Asia without permanent theaters. Troupes perform in temporary bamboo structures set up in an open field, as a rule near a Buddhist temple. The structures are used for a few days or a week and then taken down and moved to the next town, where the troupe plays again. A roof of woven mats keeps the heat in during the chilly nights, but is useless against rain. These theaters can be huge, seating 3,000 or more. Cheap seats are no more than straw mats spread on the ground in the middle of the building. You will want to go first class and reserve a canvas deck chair, surely the most sensibly comfortable way ever devised to see a play. The chairs are arranged along the sides of the theater. Put a thermos of coffee and some sandwiches by your side (your hotel can provide), stretch out luxuriously, and you are ready for the night. Be sure to book your seat at the theater in the afternoon. You need two tickets, one general admission, and one reserved seat. Performance begins around 8:00 P.M. and lasts until 6:00 or 7:00 A.M. It gets cold at night, even in tropical Burma, so wear a jacket or sweater and borrow a blanket from your hotel.

SEASON. Theater activity is highly seasonal. November through April is the cool, dry season when troupes (mostly Zat Pwe and Yokthe Pwe) perform almost every night as they travel from town to town in the central plains between Rangoon and Mandalay. The theater season is at its peak in February. When the rains begin in May troupes disband, and from July through September—Buddhist Lent—performances are not allowed.

FESTIVALS. The majority of performances of all kinds are held in conjunction with religious festivals. Therevada (Hinayana) Buddhist holidays are major occasions in the countryside and in cities alike. In Rangoon or Mandalay look for several troupes in different locations, performing three or four nights or for as long as a week during: Thadingyut, or Festival of Lights, during the full moon of the tenth lunar month, marking a joyous end to Buddhist Lent; Tazaundain, or Festival of Lights, during the full moon of the eleventh lunar month; Tabodwe, Harvest Festival, during the full moon of the second lunar month; and Thingyan, Water Festival, usually occurring in April. Troupes also perform in Rangoon January 4, Independence Day. On February 12, Union Day, groups of dancers from the provinces and hills converge on the capital. Each Buddhist temple has an annual temple festival as well. Locate one and you probably will also have located a play.

TRANSPORTATION. For the past several years a Burmese visa has been good for a maximum of seven days, with no extension allowed for any reason.

Slow boat-trips up the Irrawaddy River to Mandalay of years past aren't possible on this time schedule, but daily air flights put Rangoon just a few hours away from Mandalay, Pegu, and Pagan (the latter two famous for their pagodas, not for theater). In town, hotel taxis with English-speaking drivers, by the day or by the trip, are reliable but expensive. Or, have your destination written in Burmese script and hail a passing three-wheeler—metered and very cheap. Don't be deterred if you locate a performance 10 or even 50 miles out of town. Hire a car for the night. The roads are good, travel is safe, cost is moderate. There are city buses, but the system is not easy to decipher in a few days.

INFORMATION. There are no English newspapers. Tourist Burma often has information on performances, or ask your hotel manager. Burmese love theater and you are more likely here than in most countries to find people who can tell you instantly what troupe is playing at what temple and when.

WHAT TO SEE

A performance of any kind is a *pwe*. *Anyein Pwe*†† are variety performances of music, both Western popular and traditional, dancing, and comedy skits. *Pya Zat*††, a so-called contemporary dance-play, in fact is set in the past, usually in a magical kingdom inhabited by wizards and demons who are eventually overcome by a hero-prince. It is, however, contemporary in style as compared to the *Zat Pwe*†††, traditional dance-drama, based on legendary themes and performed to the accompaniment of a traditional orchestra of various drums, tuned gongs, cymbals, bells, oboes, and xylophones. The semicircular set of nine tuned drums played during Zat Pwe is found nowhere else in Asia. A mixed cast of actors and actresses speak, sing, and dance—an enormous challenge. High point of a play occurs about 2:30 in the morning. If you are still awake then you will see the stars of the troupe show off their skill in singing and dancing. The leading actor will sing a short line or two of lyric, followed by a burst of brilliant and difficult dancing that lasts 20 or 30 seconds. Then the lead actress will do her turn. On and on it goes until clowns, too, join in. If nine hours of playing time is too much for you, this is the time you shouldn't miss.

The dance seen in Zat Pwe is a fusion of Burmese dance, classical Thai dance introduced into Burma in 1776, and, believe it or not, Western ballet learned from the British. The typical asymmetrical torso, turned out elbows, rhomboidal leg posture, and flowing hand movements of Southeast Asian dance is joined by the leaps and turns (and dancing slippers) of Western ballet. Special melodies indicate the entrance of a prince, a love scene, a departure, and the like. Actors think nothing of improvising during performances.

The stories are romantic comedies; there is no discernible message, although Burma's government is socialist. In contrast to most popular dramatic forms in Asia, Zat Pwe contains little fighting. Its heroes are genial princes whose typical response to a problem is infectious laughter. In other parts of Asia two or three clowns suffice; in Zat Pwe eight, nine, or ten clowns hold the stage in sequence, and they are usually superb performers. An average Zat Pwe troupe will have 100 or more members who will perform during the evening both a Pya Zat and a Zat Pwe play, in that order. Stars are idolized throughout the country. Major troupes are: Kenneth Po Sein Troupe, Shwe Mandhabin Zat Pwe Troupe, and Shweman Tin Maung Zat.

Yokthe Pwe††, Burma's marionette play, has a history that goes back five hundred years. *Ramayana* stories (see **India**) are often performed. A tra-

Burmese string marionettes used for Rama plays: the demon Ravana in the form of a hermit, and Prince Rama.

ditional puppet set contains 28 doll figures: spirit votaress, king, prince, clowns, ogres, and animals. Dramatic content is simple, but the technique of manipulation by as many as 60 strings is extraordinarily complicated; a puppet may be moved through dance steps so subtle that it is said human performers learn by watching the puppets. Yokthe Pwe is not widely performed any more but occasionally still can be seen at temple festivals.

Even more difficult to see are *Nat Pwe*††, or "spirit medium dances," ritual performances in which a dance medium contacts and seeks guidance from an animistic spirit. They are not intended for the public.

Court masked dance-drama, *Zat Gyi*††††, flourished from the mid-eighteenth to the mid-nineteenth century under the patronage of Burmese kings. With the establishment of British rule in 1885 the kings lost their power, and the art declined. Plays are based on the *Ramayama* and other classical epics. Public performances today are rare.

WHERE TO GO

RANGOON. Burma's capital and largest city, Rangoon is also headquarters for most Zat Pwe troupes, and the most convenient place to look for performances. If you can, try to be in Rangoon during one of the Buddhist festival days mentioned before. Yokthe Pwe, Zat Pwe, and Anyein Pwe troupes set up their stages near the famous Shwedegon Pagoda for the annual temple festival in late February. In late November the Shweokgu Pagoda sponsors major Zat Pwe performances for four or five nights. The temple is in Thaketa, 8 miles out of Rangoon and easy to reach by taxi.

You can buy papier-mâché replicas of Zat Gyi dance masks, drums, and gongs at stalls along the stairs leading to the Shwedegon Pagoda. Bargain for the price. Theater dance costumes are sold at embroidery shops on A Road between 78th and 80th streets. There is a fairly interesting exhibit of puppets and musical instruments on the first floor of the National Museum (26 Pansodan Street; open daily except Friday).

Normally, I do not recommend hotel shows, but programs of classical Burmese performing arts at the elegant Inya Lake Hotel are worth attending; moderate charge; inquire at the hotel or Tourist Burma for dates and hours. Visitors are welcome to watch students rehearsing classical music and dance play at the State School of Music and Drama (Jubilee Hall on Shwedegon Pagoda Road) weekdays, November through May. No prior arrangements are required.

Books to Read

GENERAL: Htin Aung, *Burmese Drama* (London: Oxford University Press, 1937); James R. Brandon, *Theatre in Southeast Asia* (Cambridge, Mass.: Harvard University Press, 1967); Kenneth Sein and Joseph Withey, *The Great Po Sein* (Blooming-ton, Indiana: Indiana University Press, 1965).

PLAYS: Pok Ni, *Konmara Pya Zat: An Example of Popular Burmese Drama* (London: Luzac, 1952).

Cambodia

ambodia is a small country; yet kings of the Khmer empire (802–1431) ruled over a great part of mainland Southeast Asia. These kings built awe-inspiring temples at their capitals around Angkor—Angkor Wat, the Baphuon, the Bayon, Banteay Srei, and scores of others. A classical Khmer dance style of stunning purity developed from court performances and from religious dances of maidens dedicated to the Angkor temples. Khmer dance and its lovely accompanying *pin peat* instrumental music took root in neighboring cultures and their legacy is recognizable in the classic theater of Thailand, Laos, and Burma. To see Cambodian classic female dance-drama, male masked-plays, or shadow-drama is to be transported to this ancient age. A popular theater exists as well.

A landlocked country, off the usual through-Asia route and overshadowed by its larger neighbors, Thailand and Vietnam, Cambodia has always been an unusual destination for travelers. For a select few, a visit to the temple ruins in the jungles at Angkor was a special pilgrimage; if you were lucky you could see a performance of the Royal Cambodian Ballet troupe outdoors with Angkor Wat itself as a backdrop. Angkor is near Siem Reap and 150 miles northwest of Phnom Penh. Even fewer visitors ever made the side trip to Battambang, 50 miles west of Angkor, where an all-male temple troupe performed masked-plays and shadow-drama. When classic plays were performed at the former royal palace in Phnom Penh attendence was limited to royal guests; tourists were not included. In spite of the superlative quality of classic Cambodian theater—without argument the most exquisite in Southeast Asia—it is better known in the West by reputation than by experience.

THEATERGOING

Classical dance-drama is performed for special occasions—state holidays, national day, and for state guests. Occasional public performances also are held. Popular theater troupes perform nightly in Phnom Penh and in major provincial cities in permanent, if dirty and unpleasant, theater buildings. Tickets normally are purchased at the window. Language of all performances is Cambodian. It is too soon to know what may alter in Cambodian theater as a result of the change of government in May 1975.

SEASON. Avoid the wet season, June–August. The dry season is December–February and the best time to visit.

TRANSPORTATION. In Phnom Penh theaters are too far from hotels and the weather is too hot for walking. Order a taxi, by the day or the hour, from your hotel. Or hail a cyclo (three-wheeled bicycle) on the street; settle the fare before you go; be sure to have theater name written in Cambodian script to show your driver.

INFORMATION. No English newspapers or magazines. Do not expect to find any printed information about theater happenings. You will have to inquire. English is not widely spoken; French is.

WHAT TO SEE

Cambodia's most impressive dramatic form is *Lakon Kbach Boran*††††, an ancient classical female dance-drama. Stone inscriptions in Sanskrit tell of dancing girls attached to the king's court as early as the seventh century. During the period of the great Khmer empire six hundred dancing girls were in the service of the Baphuon Temple at Angkor. In carved reliefs on scores of temples from the Angkor period we see, in great detail, dancers (wearing flowered headdresses, diaphanous skirts, and elaborate jewelry), and gongs, tuned sets of bronze bowls, cymbals, zithers, and drums that accompanied performances. Either during the Angkor period or later (borrowed from Thailand) various legends were set to female dance, and thus Lakon Kbach Boran was born. The main plays performed today dramatize excerpts from the *Ramayana* (see **India**), the story of Prince Inao (or Panji in Java), the legend of the *Prince of the Golden Sea Shell* (*Pra Sang*), and others. Princess, queen, prince, and even demon roles are danced by women; men play religious seers and clowns (kings, played for comic effect, are clown roles). Boys play monkey roles.

In addition to hour-long dramatic episodes, the corps de ballet executes nondramatic group dances such as Tep Monoram and the Dance of the Apsaras. Costuming is exceptionally beautiful; dancers are literally sewn into formfitting silk bodices and pleated skirts. Real diamonds, rubies, and emeralds sparkle from headdresses, bracelets, and necklaces. The solid white makeup (to mask expression) of past centuries has given way to natural makeup, allowing innocently bewitching smiles to peep through. Tall spiked crowns, shoulder epaulettes, and heavily embroidered cloth are indications of nineteenth-century Thai influence.

Lakon Kbach Boran is a ballet performed to songs with dialogue. Watch for the difference between pantomimic movement that expresses the meaning of song lyrics (sung by a seated female chorus) and the graceful patterns of pure dance that have no meaning and are accompanied by rippling cascades of sound from the pin peat orchestra of bamboo xylophones, sets of tuned

A leading dancer of the Khmer classical ballet troupe as an Apsaras, or heavenly nymph, costumed after carvings on Angkor Wat.

bronze bowls, drums, bell cymbal, and oboe. Note how arms, legs, torso, and head move in sinuously interconnected and continuous patterns, feet gently touching the floor, the body seeming to float in the air. As a result of years of special exercises, elbows articulate backwards in startling fashion, as do fingers when forming seven basic hand positions (adapted from the twenty-five of Indian dance). You wonder if such an incredibly gentle, decorous dance vision can last; then the clowns enter and pratfalls and raucous, disrespectful, ad libbed patter shatter the mood.

The nationally organized Khmer Classic Ballet troupe, formerly the Royal Cambodian Ballet, is the only group to perform Lakon Kbach Boran. It is managed by the University of Fine Arts in Phnom Penh. It consists of a score of musicians, 26 teachers (former dancers), the dance company of 80 women, and about 400 students, the youngest of whom are four or five years old. Unfortunately, this superlatively trained troupe rarely appears in public and the chances of your running into a performance are regrettably slight.

Lakon Khol (or *Khol*)††† is a dramatic masked pantomime performed by men only. Episodes are taken from the *Ramayana*; especially popular are the kidnapping of Sita and the epic's final battle scenes. The dancers, who are all masked, move in vigorous, even rough, style to verses and dialogue chanted by two narrators who stand by the side of the stage with the pin peat orchestra. You will hear no songs, but some of the instrumental melodies are the same as those heard in female Lakon Kbach Boran. Khol is a parallel form to Khon masked pantomime in Thailand, and the two are extremely similar. Two temple-based troupes exist, one at Battambang and the other at the Wat Sway Temple near Phnom Penh. Performances are rare. Khol had been a royal art, but that ceased abruptly around one hundred years ago when the chief narrator and troupe head in a fit of anger kicked one of the king's favorite wives. He was instantly banished from the city and Khol hasn't been performed at court since.

Nang Sbek (sometimes *Sbek Thom*)††† is a shadow-play using enormous cutout leather puppets. Like Khol, scenes from the *Ramayana* are dramatized, two narrators declaim the same epic verses and dialogue, and the same melodies of the pin peat orchestra indicate marches, battles, love scenes, or entrances. Unusual among Asian shadow-plays, a Nang Sbek puppet— measuring five feet wide and as much as six feet high—can portray a whole scene showing three or four characters within a palace setting, or surrounded by trees, or on a battlefield. The scenes reproduced are based on the several miles of reliefs which encircle the base of Angkor Wat. As in a cartoon strip, a new puppet will be brought on to show each new sequence of action in a scene. There are also individual puppets of main figures: Rama, Sita, Hanuman, the seer, and others. Six to eight puppeteers, holding the puppets over their heads, dance out from behind a huge 30-foot-wide screen and and around its end until they are between the audience and the screen. You see the puppets first as shadows, then as silhouettes in the light of a blazing fire behind the screen. Puppet and puppeteer fuse into a stately dancing image. A single troupe of villagers living near Battambang preserves Nang Sbek in its ancient form. You can't see the villagers but you might have the good fortune to catch an occasional performance by the troupe of young dancer-puppeteers attached to the University of Fine Arts in Phnom Penh. The university troupe studied under the Battambang villagers; its style of dance is somewhat more refined than the plain village style; the troupe is quite good.

Lakon Bassak †† is the popular theater of Cambodia. It was created 60 years ago by Cambodians living in the southern part of Vietnam along the Bassak River, hence its name. Cambodian and Vietnamese elements mix: prince and

A large Nang Sbek shadow-puppet posed to show in clear detail a scene from the *Ramayana*: the monkey Angkut rejoices, holding aloft the head of Ravana's slain son, Indrajit.

princess dress in Cambodian traditional costume while the villain wears Chinese-Vietnamese costume. A clown has a Vietnamese white butterfly-patch over eyes and nose. Dances are popularized versions of Lakon Kbach Boran accompanied by traditional pin peat music; songs are sung to strings and cymbals heard in Vietnam. Plays are based on traditional legends and *Jataka* Buddhist birth-stories. A very popular dramatic form throughout Cambodia; normally a score of professional troupes play in permanent theater buildings in Phnom Penh (Krom Silpea Khmer Selai, Phsar Silep, and Rastea Chantrey), Battambang, Siem Reap, Takeo, and other provincial towns.

Chinese opera in Teochew, Hokkien, and Cantonese dialects is performed on Chinese New Year (February).

Molière and other French playwrights are staged occasionally. A modern drama section of the University of Fine Arts gives instruction in Western drama and there are occasional student performances of translations of Western drama and of newly written plays in Cambodian.

WHERE TO GO

PHNOM PENH. In recent years three commercial Lakon Bassak theaters have been open intermittently. By good fortune you might, just possibly, encounter a performance of one of the classical dramatic forms at the Theatre Municipal.

A small collection of dance masks, costumes, and shadow puppets can be seen at the National Museum, near the Grand Palace. Les Corporations Cambodgiennes, just behind the Museum, is a national organization that encourages traditional artists. For sale are papier-mâché dance masks, rubbings of stone reliefs from Angkor depicting Apsaras dancing nymphs, and models of pin peat instruments superbly cast in bronze.

There is a 2,000-foot fresco of the *Ramayana* story painted on the walls of the outer gallery that encircles the Silver Pagoda, next to the Grand Palace. Sections are in bad condition, but it is of interest because figures are modeled on Lakon Kbach Boran and Nang Sbek figures.

Grand Palace***. Formerly the Royal Palace; once under the administration of UNESCO. In years past was the site of command performances of Lakon Kbach Boran and more recently the place the public was allowed to watch rehearsals of the troupe. Today, depending upon the exigencies of the current military and political situation, the palace may or may not be open to the public. Rehearsals may or may not be held—for the same reasons. If you are seriously interested you can inquire; you will need special permission to attend. If rehearsals are held, youngsters will be training in the large open-sided pavilion about two hundred yards inside the palace entrance on the left, and the adult dancers will be using the spacious Public Tribune (over the entrance to the palace) where royalty used to appear before the public.

Krom Silpea Khmer Selai (Selai Khmer Arts Theater)**. Largest of the city's Lakon Bassak theaters. Home of the Bac Sen Bassak troupe, one of the best commercial troupes. Seats 800; moderately comfortable wicker chairs; overhead fans; hordes of mosquitoes. Acting is fairly good and spirited; drop-and-roll scenery handles 50–60 scenes of each play; traditional music; a different play each night.

Phsar Silep (Fine Arts Market)*. A miserable commercial Lakon Bassak theater; filthy and, in spite of overhead fans, hot. Seats 450 on hard chairs and benches. Actors and actresses are so bad that audience babble drowning out their voices seems a blessing.

Rastea Chantrey (Moon Queen)*. Another terrible commercial Lakon Bassak theater; dirty, smelly, hot, and unpleasant. Seats 800; front-row chairs are comfortable. Though the cast is mediocre the audience screams its delight; mikes swish through the air to follow stage action; the public-address system is deafening; a prince making love to a princess checks his wristwatch; scenery changes at the shrill blast of a whistle; a blaring trumpet and an out-of-tune piano join pin peat music in a dance scene. It's a wild place indeed.

Theatre Municipal***. New, modern, delightful theater building owned and operated by the city of Phnom Penh. Octagonal in shape, auditorium is

Theater in the Grand Palace, Phnom Penh, Cambodia.

paneled in warm wood; shallow orchestra means audience is close to very wide stage. Seats 900; air-conditioned; comfortable plush seats; all seats reserved. Excellent troupes of the University of Fine Arts perform Lakon Kbach Boran, Nang Sbek, Lakon Bassak, and Yeekay, a folk drama, for the public.

Book to Read

James R. Brandon, *Theatre in Southeast Asia* (Cambridge, Mass.: Harvard University Press, 1967).

China (Taiwan)

T he island of Taiwan, or Formosa, has been an independent kingdom, a Japanese colony, and a province of China. When it became the seat of the government of the Republic of China in 1949 and when traditional opera was gradually banned on the mainland, the island became a last preserve for old-style Chinese opera performance. A good part of this opera activity, in Mandarin and in various mainland dialects, takes place in public theaters conveniently located in the capital city of Taipei. The average quality of performance is moderately high, though rarely outstanding. Festival performances of local Taiwanese opera and children's puppet plays occur in large numbers outside Taipei in the countryside and in provincial towns. Modern drama is of little importance; amateur performances can be seen from time to time. This is the not too exciting Taiwanese theater scene.

THEATERGOING

Usually some type of Chinese opera plays nightly at one or more public theaters, 7:30 P.M.; occasional weekend matinees at 2:00–2:30 P.M. Tickets are not more than one U.S. dollar. Almost no theater is completely sold out, but to get good seats, buy a day in advance at the box office. Theater buildings are moderately good; none in Taipei is physically uncomfortable. Usually no English-language program available. Outside of Taipei you have to hunt for performance sites; rural troupes are constantly on the go from town to town. Wednesday, Saturday, and Sunday look for traditional opera on television.

SEASON. Winter is the most active season, but Taiwan's theater season hasn't the highs and lows found in other countries. The mild, semitropical climate allows theater most of the year.

FESTIVALS. As in other countries, plays are often performed in the grounds of a Buddhist temple on festival days. Look and listen for plays in progress, especially on nights of the full moon (the fifteenth day of the lunar month) in any of Taiwan's cities. In Taipei watch for Taiwanese opera and puppet plays during the full moon of the first lunar month (February) and the second lunar month (March), and for Peking opera the third lunar month (April) at Fao An Kung Temple (61 Ha Mi Street).

TRANSPORTATION. Travel is easy and distances short in Taiwan. Metered taxis cruise Taipei; there are lots of them and the cost is moderate. From downtown hotels you can easily walk to the two most active theaters, World of Today Recreation Center and Kuo Chung Wen Yi Ho-tung Chung Shin. Street signs are in Chinese characters only. A good rail line runs down the west coast connecting the major provincial cities Taichung, Tainan, and Kaohsiung with Taipei; the trip takes only a few hours. Domestic air flights reach most parts of the island.

INFORMATION. It is hit-and-miss finding out what is going on. It is strange, considering the large number of foreign visitors that pass through Taiwan, that there is no dependable weekly tourist guide in English. Two English papers, the *China Post* and the *China News,* list some plays. The TV log in the *News* lists opera programs. Front pages of the monthly *Echo* magazine describe important festivals and list, if not all, at least some, opera and puppet performances for the month.

WHAT TO SEE

Sung drama, or opera, has been the major form of Chinese drama for fifteen hundred years. Strong similarities exist in the many regional forms that grew up over the vast area of China. The essence of all Chinese opera is that it fuses song, music, dance, mime, speech, and symbolic representation into a single indivisible artistic expression. You will have no trouble recognizing the four basic role types: maidens and young scholars sing long and complex solos (there are no choruses or even duets in Chinese opera); white-faced clowns joke and go through fantastically skilful scenes of mime and acrobatics; and the powerful "painted face" characters, gods and generals, strut about the stage and battle impressively, though their voices may not be too impressive when they sing. Each spoken or sung line is accompanied by stylized, often symbolic, gestures. Imaginary doors are opened or closed and thresholds stepped over. To circle the stage is to symbolically complete a journey. A whole scene can be wordless mime: a gentle maiden shooing chickens, threading a needle, sewing her slipper; or an old man poling his boat through bouncing rapids, whirling and turning, and finally gliding safely into quiet waters. Through movement the performer's body suggests the whole physical world around it. Or, a waving blue banner is water, four vertical banners are an army, flags with embroidered wheels are a carriage. Bare of scenery and properties except for a table and two chairs, the stage in Chinese opera is a platform, no more, for an imaginary world the performers create. Curtained doorways at the rear of the stage are for entrance (right) and exit (left). As if to compensate for the utter simplicity of scenic technique,

A battle scene from *The White Snake*, a Chinese opera in Kun Ch'u style, at Today's World, Taipei. The White Snake and her opponent simultaneously hurl batons at each other.

costumes and makeup are brilliant and elaborately varied: eight-foot-long pheasant feathers bob and curl over warriors' heads; bold patterns of solid red, gold, black, green, blue, and white makeup obliterate facial features; gowns of embroidered silk have trailing "water sleeves" that float expressively through the air.

Out-of-work literati composed poignant dramas about emperors and bandits alike during the foreign Yuan dynasty (1280–1368); how the plays were performed, we don't know. After 1600, plays intended to be sung in the gentle style called *K'un Ch'u*†††† were composed by the hundreds in southern China; 40–60 acts long, they took days to get through and they were written

Kun Ch'u actress, wearing the costume and long pheasant feathers of a warrior, sings before a battle.

in difficult literary language. Scenes from K'un Ch'u, in their original musical style with soft flute melodies, are sometimes still performed.

A more popular, simpler type of opera developed in the eighteenth and nineteenth centuries in the streets and at the imperial court in Peking; hence its name *Ching Hsi*†††, "Peking," or "Capital" opera. Elements of several northern opera styles combined in Ching Hsi. The language of performance is Mandarin, the standard or national language, and gradually Ching Hsi became China's "national" dramatic form. Ching Hsi music assaults the ears with deafening cymbal and gong crashes, a machine-gun tattoo of stick upon wood-block; harsh sounds of bowed strings seem to lacerate the flesh; the solo human voice cuts through the din like a scalpel. Traditionally, the Ching Hsi singer, like the American musical-comedy performer, relied upon clarity, power, brassy tones, and just plain zing to reach his tired businessman audience. (Until this century there were no actresses.) The audience of shopkeepers came to a teahouse theater in the middle of the day for a short time to relax and catch part of a play. The singer had to work hard to get this raucous audience's attention. As few people saw a whole play, highlights from several plays came to make up a bill. Few plays were written especially for Ching Hsi; rather, managers adapted old favorites to the racy new music and actors ad libbed without bothering to learn dialogue or even song lyrics. Important in introducing Ching Hsi to American and European audiences was the great female impersonator Mei Lan Fang, who toured the West in the 1920s and 1930s. Today actresses play female roles and the impersonator is a thing of the past.

Ching Hsi is performed in Taiwan, primarily by and for refugees from northern China. Important troupes are sponsored by the army, navy, and air force (theater: Kuo Chung Wen Yi Ho-tung Chung Shin); their best performers, who left mainland China in 1949–1950, are now reaching retirement age. A commercial troupe of younger players performs at World of Today. The Foo Hsing Opera School in suburban Taipei gives occasional performances; their children's troupe has toured the United States.

Ching Hsi's popularity is limited to the minority of Taiwanese who have learned Mandarin in school and to the newly arrived northern Chinese. The local Taiwanese population attends *Ko-tsai-hi*†, "Taiwanese opera." Less stylized than Ching Hsi, simpler, and somewhat modernized, Ko-tsai-hi is a rather crude but very popular form. About 40–50 commercial troupes are on the island. Several used to perform in Taipei nightly but the theaters are now torn down. To see Ko-tsai-hi you will need to find a temple performance in Taipei, or go to Taichung, Tainan, or other provincial cities to seek out the ramshackle commercial theaters where troupes still play. Opera in several other Chinese dialects is occasionally performed.

To my ear, the most attractive of all Chinese opera forms is Honanese opera†††. The music is ravishingly, hauntingly melodic; acting is deeply emotional, remarkably genuine in feeling, and compelling. I once caught a whole week of Honanese opera; it simply bowled me over. Performances are rare in Taiwan but you might be lucky.

Local Taiwanese *Po-the-hi*†, glove-puppet plays, are performed in temple courtyards and in the streets. It is said three hundred troupes roam the island. They play three or four days in one location before moving on to the next. Two puppeteers, three musicians, and a couple of flash-powder technicians combine forces. Children love the crude, knockabout, blood-and-thunder tales of heroic warriors pitted against frightening monsters. Prettied-up versions are put on television each week, too.

College students perform *Hua Ju*††, "talking plays," modeled on modern Western drama. There are no professional, or semiprofessional, modern drama troupes. Tight censorship in the Republic of China does not encourage writers to grapple with contemporary social, let alone political, issues in the drama. Hua Ju was a vital force in China during the first half of this century; it is of little significance in Taiwan today. Second-rate musical variety shows run at one or two theaters in Taipei, mostly following the sexless approach of Japanese musicals.

WHERE TO GO

TAIPEI. The city has half-a-dozen theaters; some are new and several are open most nights. It is the place to begin theatergoing in Taiwan. Most people will not find it worthwhile to look further, for entertainments of the country-side are scarcely of high artistry.

Kuo Chung Wen Yi Ho-tung Chung Shin (Armed Forces Cultural Activities Center)**. A bare-bones, functional hall; conveniently located; seats 950 in well-raked orchestra and small balcony. Vinyl covered, soft seats are fairly comfortable; air-conditioned; Chinese-language program. Song text in Chinese characters is projected on the side of the stage, just in case you can read but cannot speak Chinese. Military troupes, usually excellent, perform here several nights each week. Not advertised in English papers. To find out what is playing go to the box office and corral a bystander to translate for you; buy your ticket in advance.

Kuo Fu Chi-nien Kuan (Sun Yat-sen Memorial Hall, also National Memorial Hall)****. Taipei's prestige theater; built by the government in 1972. A single, monolithic, blocklike structure, overwhelming from the out-side; spacious and severely conceived interior. In awesomely towering 100-foot-high lobby is a massive Lincoln-like statue of Dr. Sun Yat-sen. Dining rooms, conference rooms, and exhibition halls in addition to 2,875-seat theater. Amphitheater seating rises in steeply-raked, curving rows; comfortable seating in wide chairs; air-conditioned; no balcony. Auditorium is so large you need to sit close or bring binoculars. Semicircular stage, 80 feet in diameter, thrusts into auditorium. Too large for traditional opera or modern drama but fine for orchestral or dance concerts. Chinese-language program. Rents to various groups. Student performances of Ching Hsi some Saturday afternoons.

Kuo Li Yi-shu Kuan (National Arts Hall)**. An older building seating 600 in well-raked orchestra and three-row balcony. Narrow and uncomfortable seats; noisy with passing traffic; air-conditioned. Rented by young amateur modern-drama groups, and for music concerts for the most part. Program may be printed in English.

Oscar Music Hall. Seats 400 in upholstered lounge chairs; flat orchestra floor, narrow balcony goes around three sides. Air-conditioned; oldish; high stage. This is a sort of modern teahouse presenting a three-a-day variety show of modern songs, dances, and a few sketches, with free tea at your seat. Show is a copy of a Japanese copy of an American variety show and pretty dull stuff.

Taiwan Television, Studio #5 *. Many Ching Hsi telecasts originate here. Seats 200 on one level in lovely, warm, intimate atmosphere; plush seats; air-conditioned; foreign spectators uncommon. Must obtain special pass from studio to attend once or twice weekly live telecasts. Absolutely no talking, no photography, no taping.

World of Today Recreation Center *. A building containing restaurants, massage parlors, pinball rooms; two theaters are open nightly through the year. A permanent troupe, mostly young players, does Ching Hsi (and occasionally K'un Ch'u) in **Giraffe Hall**, fourth floor. Seats 600 in well-raked orchestra; no balcony; large, soft chairs; air-conditioned; pleasant atmosphere. As in the old teahouses, tea is brought gratis to your chair. Full-length plays in the evening; in serial form they may extend over 10–15 nights. The audience of fanatical fans, mostly old men, knows the operas by heart. Can be SRO; wise to phone for reservation. Skilled, but not first-rate performances. Also, one-hour daily matinees of Ching Hsi for foreign audiences; the bill of five or six excerpts changes monthly. Look for ad in English-language newspapers; program printed in English; translation of song lyrics projected on screen. No reservation necessary; audience is rarely larger than 40–50. Can photograph and tape record. This is a good introduction to Chinese opera; lots of acrobatics and mime; interesting costumes and makeup. An all-girl song and dance troupe performs in the sixth floor theater. Seats 800 in raked orchestra; comfortable seats; air-conditioned. Three shows a day. Cast frantically dashes through 30 numbers in two hours.

Production is slick and pretty; emotionless, doll-like girls. Loudspeakers placed all through the house bombard you with singers' voices; it's all lip-sync, and eerily nary a sound comes from the stage itself.

Books to Read

GENERAL: Elizabeth Halson, *Peking Opera: A Short Guide* (London: Oxford University Press, 1966); Colin P. Mackerras, *The Rise of the Peking Opera, 1770–1870* (Oxford: Clarendon Press, 1972); A. C. Scott, *The Classical Theatre of China* (London: Allen and Unwin, 1967); Cecilia S. L. Zung, *Secrets of the Chinese Drama* (New York: Benjamin Blom, 1964).

PLAYS: Cyril Birch, *Anthology of Chinese Literature* (New York: Grove Press, 1965); Josephine Hung Huang, *Children of the Pear Garden* (Taipei: Heritage Press, 1961); A. C. Scott, *Traditional Chinese Plays*, 3 vols. (Madison, Wisc.: University of Wisconsin Press, 1967–1975).

Hong Kong

N o one goes to Hong Kong to see theater. Business, not arts, is the Crown Colony's strong suit. Still, you might be surprised to know that you can see traditional Chinese opera and modern Chinese drama. Even though the population is 95 percent Chinese, British cultural influence is strong, and you can attend Western amateur drama, concert music, and ballet. The thing about Hong Kong is that it is convenient: it seems that everyone traveling through Asia stops here; it is small and it is incredibly easy to get around in; things work; the climate is moderate; even American English is understood; and ticket prices are ridiculously low for a developed area. Professional theater is a rarity, but a good deal of low profile semi-professional theater activity has grown up in recent years. A stimulus has been City Hall Theatre, on Hong Kong Island, built by the government and opened to local and foreign groups a decade ago. A new Kowloon Cultural Complex is scheduled to be built by 1980 on a site next to the Kowloon Railway Station. When completed it will contain a 2,500-seat concert hall, a 1,000-seat theater, an art gallery, a planetarium, and a museum. If Hong Kong's theater arts still are nothing very much to brag about, the situation is better than it was in the past.

THEATERGOING

SEASON. Winter (November–February) is the busiest theater time. The weather is the best then, too.

FESTIVALS. You can see traditional Chinese opera in the streets and in commercial theaters to celebrate major Chinese festivals. Important festivals are: the lunar New Year (February), the Dragon Boat Festival (June), and Mid-autumn Festival (September–October). On Cheung Chau Island (30 minutes by ferry) on the third night of the Festival of the Buns, Chinese opera is performed all night; usually in May; very crowded. In odd-numbered years, the government sponsors the Festival of Hong Kong, ten days in November–December, during which operas and dances are staged outdoors near City Hall and in other locations. All events are free and listed in the special Festival Program, sold at tourist agencies. Nightly performances of plays, concerts, operas, and dance highlight the Hong Kong Arts Festival for four jam-packed weeks each February. At City Hall; mostly foreign invited groups; invariably SRO; buy tickets in advance.

TRANSPORTATION. Both the mainland Kowloon side of the city and Hong Kong Island are small enough to make walking a pleasure. Detailed maps are easy to obtain. You will love the double-decker buses. Cruising metered taxis are cheap. Star Ferry links Kowloon and Victoria in a delightful 15-minute trip that costs pennies.

INFORMATION. Go straight to the office of the Hong Kong Tourist Association at Star Ferry Terminal, Kowloon. They will give you maps, *Hong Kong Official Guide* (with a monthly calendar of events), and a copy of City Hall Theatre schedule (all free). You will find some music and drama listings in weekly *What's Doing in Hong Kong*; not much appears in English-language newspapers, except ads for hotel shows—which I don't recommend.

WHAT TO SEE

The most commonly performed type of Chinese opera in Hong Kong is "Cantonese opera," sung in the southern Chinese dialect spoken by most people in Hong Kong. *Kwangtung Hsi*†† follows many basic conventions of traditional Chinese opera (see **China**), combining singing with stylized movements and gestures. Its music is considered light and popular, not classical; symbolism is slight; melodies are soft and romantic, rather than strident as in northern opera forms; there are no acrobatics; costumes are gaudy with glittering sequins; performers move through three-dimensional painted sets. Several professional troupes perform regularly. (Theater: Lai Chi Kok Amusement Park.) Lung Cheung Opera Company was established by Radio Hong Kong in 1967 to set a professional standard.

Ching Hsi, the northern China opera form (see **China**) sung in Mandarin, is infrequently staged; the Mandarin-speaking population of Hong Kong is small. There is no professional Ching Hsi group; troupes like the Chun Chau Chinese Operatic School, the Ching Fung Opera Research Group, or the

An important official in Ching Hsi opera. The painted
face indicates that he has a strong temperament; the
whip, that he is on horseback.

Lui Cheung Lun are semiprofessional. Children's troupes, trained by these
groups, often perform.

Among the small number of amateur modern-drama groups in Hong Kong,
Theatre for All, which performs in Cantonese, and the old-line British Stage
Club, which performs in English, are well-known.

WHERE TO GO

City Hall ****. In the British sense, this is the municipal auditorium of
Hong Kong, containing a library, museum, art galleries, conference rooms,

City Hall, Hong Kong.

clubrooms, a 1,500-seat **Concert Hall** and a 500-seat **Theatre**. A modern air-conditioned cultural complex; conveniently located next to Star Ferry Terminal on Hong Kong Island. Comfortable seats; well-raked auditoriums for good viewing; excellent acoustics. Good restaurant, bars, and lounges. Free English-language program. Monthly schedule is posted in many hotels. Virtually every night, one or the other theater will be open for some performance: Western opera, the Hong Kong Philharmonic Orchestra, vocal concerts, or a visiting foreign dance or music group in the Concert Hall; modern Cantonese or English drama, Chinese opera, variety shows, and student programs in the Theatre. The best performances are those sponsored by the Urban Council (and are so noted in the schedule).

Lai Chi Kok Amusement Park**. One of the last remaining amusement parks in Asia; formerly overseas Chinese made them a part of urban life wherever they lived. It costs about a quarter to get in and there are restaurants, a zoo, a monorail, rides, games of chance, and, of course, theaters. Eight of them to be exact. Western and Chinese movies, popular singers, vaudeville, and sad strip shows (featuring "exotic" Japanese and Filipino girls) are of little interest. But in **Theatre #2** (they are numbered) you can see moderately good Cantonese opera every night of the year. Seats 900 on flat concrete floor. A simple shed building, not too clean; open on the sides for ventilation. You can sit in the back free; tickets for the cushioned front seats

Lai Chi Kok amusement park entrance, Hong Kong.

are sold by the right entrance to the theater. Ching Hsi is usually performed each night at **Theatre #3** (the one with the sculpted reliefs of Balinese dancing girls decorating the façade). No free seats; buy tickets at the entrance to the theater. Seats about 400; relatively pleasant and clean; not air-conditioned. No program at either theater; if you must know what is playing, ask at the ticket booth and you might be lucky enough to find someone who speaks English. The park is crowded on weekends but not otherwise. A gaudy, slightly sleazy, but above-board place.

Books to Read

See **China**.

India

The most challenging of all Asian countries for the theatergoer. More than forty distinct dramatic forms are tantalizingly scattered over a vast area, in teeming metropolises and in remote and seldom visited villages. The amount and range of theater is overwhelming and the main problem is to decide where to begin. No single city is the theater center of India, as Tokyo is of Japan; there is no one place where you can see most of what you would like to see. Instead, there are more than a dozen major regions, each with its own language, its regional capital, and its regional dramatic forms. A world-famous form like Kathakali is seldom seen outside its own region. Theatergoing in India is a bit like prospecting for gold: you have to travel far and wide; you have to search endlessly; you have to be ready to sift through dross. As with gold, it is the excitement of the hunt and the richness of the find that makes it all worthwhile.

Behind the multiplicity of Indian theater forms lies a number of common cultural and artistic principles, however. The majority of Indians practice Brahmanism (Hinduism), an ancient religion whose elaborately conceived ritual and rich legend infuse the theater. Dance and drama are described as having been created by Brahma, Vishnu, Shiva, and other Hindu gods. No traditional performance can begin without ritual offerings and prayers to the gods.

Further, two extremely long epics provide boundless dramatic material. They are the *Ramayana* and the *Mahabharata*, set down in writing from an older oral tradition, more than twenty-five hundred years ago. The *Ramayana* is a romantic chronicle of the exile of Prince Rama from the kingdom of Ayodhya and his final triumphant return to his homeland as king. Rama is banished to the forest for 13 years, accompanied by his brother Lakshmana and his wife Sita. Sita is kidnapped by the immortal demon king Ravana and carried to his capital of Lanka (Ceylon). With the help of his brother, the white monkey Hanuman, and armies of the monkey king Sugriva, Rama defeats Ravana, rescues Sita, and is crowned king of Ayodhya. To Indians, Rama represents a supreme model of princely virtue and Sita, of conjugal fidelity. Rama is worshipped as a god, for he is Vishnu's seventh incarnation.

The *Mahabharata* is four times as long as the *Ramayana* and contains thousands of episodes and hundreds of characters. Most important are the final sections recounting the War of the Bharats, in which the five noble Pandawa brothers recover the kingdom of Astina from their cousins and enemies, the ninety-nine Kurawa brothers. Chief heroes are Ardjuna and Bima, two of the Pandawa brothers; Krishna, eighth incarnation of Vishnu, is their adviser. In a well-known philosophic section, the *Bhagavad Gita*, or *Song of the Lord*, Krishna extols to Ardjuna the duty of the warrior to fight even his relations righteously, with neither malice nor pity. The epic ends when Bima kills the Kurawa king, Duryodhana, and the Pandawas assume rule of Astina. The *Ramayana*, with its chivalric and romantic overtones, its simple morality, and its focus upon a single hero and heroine, has proven somewhat more susceptible to dramatization than has the morally ambiguous and grim *Mahabharata*, with its multiple heroes and heroines. (The two epics are also dramatized in classical dramas in a dozen countries outside India.)

All Indian dramatic forms draw upon a single, composite system of bodily movement and dance. It is an ancient system, codified in writing thousands of years ago. Figures in dance poses can be seen in temple sculpture in every part of India. Its danced sign language is the world's most elaborate. Two dozen hand gestures (*hasta* or *mudra*) represent nouns, verbs, adjectives, adverbs, and other parts of speech. When a song is sung, the hands simultaneously "write" in motion the words being sung; lyrics are repeated twice, or six times, or even twenty times as the actor or actress elaborates on their meaning with ever more subtle visual images. Melody comes from plucked lute (*sarod* or *vina*) or Western violin while bell cymbals strike the beat, and drums match the dancer's flashing, stunningly complex foot movements. Virtuoso footwork is the hallmark of classical Indian dancing irrespective of the particular style.

Wherever you see Indian theater, it will be emotional, assertive, active, intensely and overtly expressive—pushing performers' bodies and voices to maximum physical effort. The Indian stage pulsates; it vibrates with energy. Elsewhere in Asia an attitude of courtly reserve binds the dancer into attitudes of restraint and repose, but in India eyes flash and limbs move without inhibition.

THEATERGOING

Quite different types of drama and different viewing conditions are found in urban and in rural India. Major urban theater centers are New Delhi, Bombay, Calcutta, and Madras. In the cities you can see popular plays, modern drama, classical dance concerts, theater festivals, regional and folk performances on certain occasions, and more rarely revivals of ancient Sanskrit drama. Most theater buildings are rented by outside groups for short runs of a few days or a week. Performances begin early, at 6:00 or 7:00 P.M., with an occasional weekend matinee. English programs are free; tickets are inexpensive; it is quite easy to reach urban playhouses. Unfortunately much of what is seen in the cities of India is not very interesting theater; major exceptions are a few excellent avant-garde drama groups and festivals to which regional folk groups are invited.

Seeing regional plays is another matter entirely. Performances can be hard to locate. They occur on certain days of the year only. With luck and planning you may be able to drop in on a splendid regional performance in a city where you happen to be staying; it can take several days to travel out and back to see a regional performance in the countryside. Be prepared for some physical discomfort. Remember, you can't see everything in one trip to India: carefully pick which regional forms you like and budget enough time to see them. They could be the highlight of your Indian stay.

THEATER BUILDINGS.   There is no four-star theater in India. In cities antique theaters remaining from colonial times and based on English models are often charming and of historic interest; there are also more recently built, comfortable, functional halls. Most state capitals have a "Tagore Theater," built with central government funds to honor, in 1961, the one-hundredth anniversary of the birth of the Nobel prizewinning playwright Rabindranath Tagore. Comfortable theaters, often air-conditioned, they lack adequate stage equipment to meet demands of most drama. Don't miss the experience in a north Indian city of watching a play in a multicolored *shamiyana* tent, pitched on someone's lawn, stage raised at one end and the rest of the grass area spread thick with oriental rugs. Regional performances are given out-of-doors on the bare earth or on improvised stages before a temple, in a school yard, or using the veranda of someone's home. It is rare in India to run across the kind of temporary bamboo and thatch structures that are common in the rural areas of Indonesia, Burma, and Thailand.

SEASON. Season is important in both cities and the countryside. The peak theater season comes during the dry winter months, October–February. Urban performances peter out during the fierce heat of April–May (it can go to 120°F) and folk performances cease entirely in the countryside from June to August when torrential monsoon rains lash all India.

FESTIVALS. Two nationwide Hindu holidays are celebrated with dances and plays in many parts of India: Holi, the Spring Festival, during the full moon of the month of Phalgun (the first lunar month, usually February) and ten-day Dusshera, or Durga's Festival, beginning the first night of the month of Asvin (the eighth lunar month, usually September–October). Christian pageant plays can be seen in Goa at Christmas and Easter. Regional performances occasioned by local religious celebrations are described later.

Secular theater festivals are organized in New Delhi by the national government's Sangeet Natak Akademi (Academy of Music, Dance, and Drama) and in the states by branches of the Akademi, by private dance and music schools, and by the nongovernment Bharatiya Natya Sangh (All India Theater Association). Be on the lookout for them; most are very good.

TRANSPORTATION. New Delhi, Bombay, Calcutta, and Madras are on international air routes and easily reached. Plan carefully your domestic flights within India and make firm reservations in advance; flights are over-booked most of the time and changing a reservation in India can be a dreadful hassle. Trains and buses are slow, if cheap, and are tolerable for short distances, but remember, India is a huge country: from Kerala to New Delhi takes five days by train and five hours by plane. Cars can be hired, with driver, for Rs 150–200 a day. Inexpensive metered taxis are plentiful in the cities; if one doesn't cruise by, hunt up a taxi stand. Drivers usually speak English. Or, for a much cheaper ride, hail a metered three-wheeler scooter-cab; driver will not speak English.

INFORMATION. Most city performances are advertised or listed in daily English-language newspapers. An ad may appear for a single day. Weekly tourist guides are seldom useful. For a complete schedule of festival performances, buy *A Calendar of Festivals of Music, Dance, and Drama*, published by and sold at the Sangeet Natak Akademi (Rabindra Bhavan, Ferozeshah Road, New Delhi). Local offices of the Sangeet Natak Akademi or of the Bharatiya Natya Sangh may be able to give information on folk performances in their region. Bookstores carry many books on Indian drama, published in English, not generally available in the West. English-language drama magazines: *Enact* and *Sangeet Natak Akademi Journal.*

WHAT TO SEE

Two thousand years ago Sanskrit drama was the pride of Indian culture. For the entertainment and spiritual elevation of patron kings, court poets wrote beautifully composed plays expressing a Hindu view of a harmonious universe in which each man and woman fulfils his or her duty. Major figures in the plays speak prose dialogue and recite poetic verses; a stage manager introduces the action; musicians accompany movements with instrumental music; special vocalists sing verses describing emotions of the characters on stage. Legendary plays, often from the *Ramayana* and *Mahabharata*, and social plays as well, exploit the emotion of love. Death is forbidden on stage. The germ of this fastidious Sanskrit drama lies in the aesthetic concept of *rasa*, "flavor": the spectator watches the playwright's well-wrought emotional scenes expressed through appropriate artistic means—acting, singing, dance, song, and visual spectacle—and as a result the spectator experiences a feeling of spiritual joy, or rasa. Originating in drama, the principle of rasa came to underlie all Indian arts. Of the thousands of Sanskrit plays written—ranging from ten-act plays to one-acters—about two dozen have come down to us. Hindu courts, which had patronized the drama, were conquered by Moslem princes; the Brahmanic plays were no longer performed; the scripts were lost. Today we do not know just how these sophisticated dramas were staged, although we have a number of hints. The parallel with the demise of Greek tragedy is striking.

Kudiyattam†††† is an archaic remnant of this ancient dramatic tradition surviving in the state of Kerala in the far south. A classical Sanskrit drama is recited line by line by actors who then explicate the meaning of the Sanskrit lines with elaborate hand and facial gesture. A single four-line verse can take an hour to perform: an act, one night, two nights, or three. Kudiyattam contains no dance; the gorgeously costumed actors often sit for hours as they gesture and speak to wailing oboes and to the hypnotically repetitious drumming of huge, clay-pot drums. Performed behind huge flaming oil lamps. Performances are extremely rare, as only a handful of actors are alive. A profoundly moving experience.

Sanskrit studies societies in Calcutta, Madras, and New Delhi occasionally stage Sanskrit plays using student actors. There is no attempt in these amateur performances to recreate ancient theatrical techniques. Sanskrit dramas are also translated into modern Indian vernaculars and staged by modern-drama groups. Nowhere, however, can you see significant reconstructions of Sanskrit drama on the stage today. What a pity.

Classical drama died in the great courts of north India after A.D. 1200. Traditional theater continued to live, however, in a dozen guises in minor courts and in villages dedicated to drama. Only a few of the many regional dramatic forms that exist can be described here. In southern India the oldest and most honored forms are dance-dramas; while claiming fidelity to ancient dramatic practice, in fact the spoken word is subservient to the danced gesture. *Kathakali* †††† of Kerala State is acted by a male cast; actors dance and mime the meaning of songs, in Malayalam vernacular, sung by two

An outdoor Kathakali performance, Guruvayur village, Kerala State. The headdress like a nimbus, green face makeup, and cheeks extended with projecting white paper identify the hero. The face of the modest heroine, played by an actor, is half hidden by the shawl.

musician-singers. Music is gong, cymbal, and two drums; the drummers play with mind-boggling speed and power. The text consists solely of songs, and the actors neither speak nor sing, relying completely on their phenomenal skill in mimetic and dance movement for expression. Towering headdresses, the boldest makeup anywhere in the world, swirling costumes, and fiercely emotional acting seen by torchlight at a temple festival make for a powerful theatrical experience.

Plays are based on episodes from the *Ramayana* and *Mahabharata* and other legendary sources. Mood ranges from tender, in a four-night romantic play about King Nala, to terrifying, when Bima, ripping entrails from an enemy, gorges on them, bloody-mouthed and demonically possessed. Kathakali derives from Kudiyattam but is easier for a popular audience to follow. It is simpler to understand and is filled with exciting action and masculine, leaping dance steps. Like Kudiyattam, its facial and hand gesture language code is impressively detailed and eye-catching. Several dozen troupes play night after night in Kerala, moving to a new location on invitation, through the winter and spring months. Recommended regional performances at Cheruthuruthy and Trivandrum. Special tourist shows are an easy way to see Kathakali (if you are in Kerala State) and are not bad: **Cultural Centre** in Cochin, nightly except Thursday year round (Kalathil Parambu Lane, Ernakulam South, behind Laxman Theatre); and **Udyogamandal**, just outside Cochin, Thursdays, October–April. Travel agents and hotels can arrange transportation and tickets.

In seldom-seen *Krishnattam*†††, also Kerala State, the story of Krishna's life is acted out in eight, night-long plays. Makeup, costumes, staging, music, and singing style are similar to Kathakali. Dance is delicate and extended, suiting the romantic and refined nature of the god Krishna. A single troupe in Guruvayur town performs on special occasions, usually in temples where non-Hindus cannot enter. An important play festival is held during Dussera.

Yakshagana††† dance-plays in the state of Mysore take up the same mythological stories as Kathakali; vigorous stick drumming is similar to Kathakali. Dance style emphasizes footwork; no codified system of hand gestures. Actors deliver extended songs and prose dialogue in Kannada vernacular. Key performer is the narrator who introduces scenes with eloquent descriptive passages. The oldest play is from 1564. In frenzied battle scenes that seem to go on for hours, the hero whirls round and round on his knees in a remarkable technical display of athletic skill. A dozen troupes perform outdoors each night during winter months, moving from village to village. Or, at indoor performances, action is eliminated and actors concentrate on song, narrative, and philosophic discourse. Recommended regional performance in Udipi.

A surge of Krishna worship swept India in the fifteenth and sixteenth centuries, giving rise to new dance and drama forms, their common theme being the passionate longing of a female devotee of Krishna for union, spiritual and physical, with the beloved godhead. By fusing the religious and the sensuous, these theatrical forms became enormously popular. *Kuchipudi*††† dance drama of Andhra Pradesh State in central India, charms you with its syncopated and catchy drum rhythms that support intricate patterns

A young actor playing a coquettish maiden in a solo Kuchipudi dance designed to demonstrate technique: the performer executes difficult dance movements while standing on the edges of a brass bowl and balancing a water pot on his head.

of the dancer's footwork. Pure dance sections are blindingly fast; the rhythm changes every few seconds. Related to classical southern dance (Bharata Natyam), its style is appealingly supple and sensual. Song melodies blend sentiment and vigor. The all-male cast is divided among actors of male and of female roles; two narrators double as stand-up comedians. Actors must be consummate artists, for each must act, speak, sing, and dance with equal skill. (I confess Kuchipudi is my favorite among Indian dance-dramas.) Many troupes performed Kuchipudi in the past; now a single troupe based in the village of Kuchipudi tours part of the year. Its star is Vedantam Satyanarayana, a superlative portrayer of Setyabhama, Krishna's seductive wife and lover. Recommended regional performance at Kuchipudi Village.

In northern India pageant plays express the people's devotion to Krishna. *Ras Lila*†† troupes are especially active in the Braj area of Uttar Pradesh State where Krishna is said to have been born. The plays enact episodes from Krishna's youth and his dalliance with love-smitten milk maids. Performance is considered a literal enactment of the god's life; the playing area is attached to a temple; spectators watch in a spirit of religious devotion, they kiss the feet of the boy actor playing Krishna, as if he were the god himself, they cry out prayers to the players. To assure purity in performance only young boys take roles. Ras Lila, "dance-and-play," consists of two parts. First, a Ras group-dance in classical Kathak style lasts about an hour; then, the Lila, or play, takes up, in simple prose dialogue and devotional songs, an episode in Krishna's life. The Lila lasts two or three hours. Performance is during the day time. Shoes must not be worn. The youth and inexperience of the boy actors prevent performance from reaching a high artistic level. Recommended regional performances, Mathura and Vrindabad.

Ram Lila †† is a spectacular pageant of the life of Rama that can continue for 30 days. A day's episode takes place in the most appropriate part of town, the audience following each day to the new stage site. Less religious in intent than Ras Lila, yet as an act of devotion an actor may play a role through his lifetime. Banaras (Varanasi) is the home of a score of Ram Lila troupes; during Dussera you will see different scenes being staged simultaneously on street corners through the city; throngs of spectators fill every available open space where there is a view of a stage. Ram Lila is a happening and a ritual. Recommended regional performances: Banaras and Allahabad.

There are shadow-plays in India, too, presumed to be very ancient. The two most developed shadow-play forms are similar: *Tholu Bomalatta*†† of Andhra Pradesh State and *Togalu Gombe Atta*†† of Mysore. Large, translucent puppets, jointed at the shoulders, wrists, hips, and knees (and sometimes the neck), are literally danced, whirled, even hurled across the white screen. The bright light casts a shadow of pure colors: green and red predominating. Four or five puppeteers, each handling one puppet, work together; three or

A boy actor in the Ram Lila at Banaras is made up for the role of Rama while a Hindu devotee sitting beside him invokes the holy name "Rama, Rama."

four other members of the troupe play harmonium, bell cymbals, gong, and drum, and sing verses to which puppets are animated. Each puppeteer speaks the dialogue of his (or her) puppet. The stories dramatized are from the *Ramayana*. Hundreds of troupes existed in the past, patronized by provincial courts and, when touring, by villagers' contributions; a handful still perform today. Almost impossible to find a performance without traveling several hundred miles to remote interior villages. In Kerala State, simple, opaque puppets, *Tholpava Koothu*†, are moved in a technique similar to Indonesian Wayang Kulit: a center stick is stuck into a hole in a board to hold the puppet. Unlike the Indonesian form, several puppeteers work simultaneously, and a row of candles lights a 15-foot playing area of the screen. *Ramayana* and *Mahabharata* plays. Troupes perform in the Trivandrum area. In Rajasthan State, string marionettes manipulated on a small proscenium stage act out Islamic tales; these troupes are very popular throughout the state.

These are all traditional dramatic forms. Other forms grew up in the nineteenth and twentieth centuries; many are in north India; they are secular and mainly urban; they reflect the beginnings of modernization in India. Some dancing can occur, but it seldom is important; these are sung plays that rely upon the actor's and actress' vocal ability. Crude clown characters are common; sexual puns abound (note the audience reaction); topics range from historical romances to contemporary husband-and-wife conflicts. Audiences come mainly from the working class; performances in small towns may draw nearby farmers as well. Performers are professionals; nightly performances are usual, often in commercial theaters; it is fairly easy to find performances in the large cities.

Jatra †† is the tremendously popular operatic form of West Bengal, Assam, Bihar, and Orissa states. Historical events, rural themes, problems of modern city life, and trenchant political criticism make up Jatra's potpourri of plays drawn from every source under the sun, including the movies. Female impersonators are major attractions of traditional all-male troupes; modernized troupes include actresses. Performance takes place on a simple raised platform placed in the center of the audience, which sits on cushions and rugs; a prompter (who follows the script and calls out lines) and musicians sit along one edge of the stage; performers may rest along the other edges; performance lasts three or four hours; exciting entrances and exits are made on rampways through the audience. Eloquence is prized, and the actor, singing or speaking, seems on the point of an emotional explosion. A score of Jatra troupes move out of Calcutta on circuit. Dussera is a good time to catch Jatra in Calcutta itself. Inquire.

On the opposite side of the country, in western India, Bhavai, Nautanki, and Tamasha troupes perform in an area that makes up a third of the subcontinent. The narrator of *Bhavai* †† links together for the audience a sequence of eight to ten independent sketches. Plays are about ordinary people whose view of life is tolerant, accepting, and positive. The stage is a circle drawn in the earth; the audience sits on the ground around it; entrances are made down a pathway which has been kept clear; torches blazing in the night light the way for the female impersonator; singers seated at the edge of the circle share with the actors lyrics of the songs; five-foot brass trumpets blare, drums thunder, and a harmonium gasps the melody. A low-class entertainment now, Bhavai performers proudly trace their art's beginning to fifteenth-century devotional songs. Performed by itinerant troupes almost exclusively in rural areas in Gujerat State, north of Bombay; very hard to find performances.

Nautanki† is a virile folk opera of the plains. It celebrates heroes of the Islamic period, deeds of religious merit, and the paradoxes of domestic relations; its plays show the characteristic mixture of Hindu and Islamic culture of northwest India. Traditionally only men perform, but actresses are increasingly accepted. Nautanki is fast paced and filled with vigorous action. You might run into one of the large professional Nautanki troupes if you are in any of the provincial cities of Uttar Pradesh, Rajasthan, or Punjab.

Tamasha†† of Maharashtra State has a bad reputation. Double-entendre lyrics and erotic dancing of Tamasha actresses draw audiences almost exclusively male. Tamasha songs have been a big source of Indian movie music; now Tamasha borrows back the movies' dreadfully sloppy songs for the stage. Four or five Tamasha troupes share a playbill; the first ones do song-and-dance routines; only the last on the bill performs a full operatic play. Tamasha troupes regularly perform in big city theaters. (Bombay: New Hanuman Theater.)

Run-down musical-drama troupes, an anachronism lingering on from the last century, can be found here and there in nooks and crannies of the vast subcontinent. *Surabhi*† troupes tour back villages in Andhra Pradesh State and occasionally Tamil Nadu State to the south. Actors and actresses belt out rasping songs in ramshackle temporary theaters for rural audiences. Four or five troupes; hard to locate, though there is no reason really to look for one. Nineteenth-century English melodrama was transplanted to India and, as *Natya*†, flourished in a dozen cities. Though virtually dead now, a few old troupes preserve a remnant of the vanished European tradition in Bombay and Madras; actors tear a passion to tatters, enter and exit to band music, and burst into ghastly singing. (Bombay: Bhang Wedi Theater.)

In recent times classical dance has been experiencing a major revival, partly as a nationalistic reaction against past British cultural domination. Dance is the best preserved of India's ancient performing arts. Small, weathered carvings of the 108 basic dance positions of classical dance can be seen at Chidambaram Temple, Tamil Nadu State; at Ramappa Temple, Andhra Pradesh State, there are exquisite larger-than-life statues of dancers carved in black stone that show each finger and curve of the body in perfect condition. During this century, a female solo style of concert-dance evolved from women's temple dancing in Tamil Nadu State. This angular and austerely elegant dance is now called *Bharata Natyam*††††. The seven standard sections of a concert illustrate: pure dance, emphasizing rhythmic footwork and drumming to the exclusion of meaning and of song; mimetic pantomine expressing through facial and hand gesture the meaning of a song without rhythm; and storytelling dance, fusing pure dance and mime. Bharata Natyam is studied widely throughout India; concerts in cities are frequent. Recommended regional performance at Music Academy, Madras, during Christmas season. Devotional ballets about Krishna, called *Kuruvanji*†††, are choreographed in Bharata Natyam style. Recommended regional performance at Kalakshetra, Madras. *Bhagavatha Mela*† is all-male religious dance-play using Bharata Natyam dance; in village of Melatur, Tamil Nadu State.

Orissi†††, also a female solo concert-dance, is an offshoot of Bharata Natyam. To the uninitiated it may be difficult to distinguish the two; Orissi dance style is curving, soft, sensuous. A delightful dance when well performed. Not seen often outside its native state of Orissa. *Kathak*††† is the classical dance of north India and can be performed by men or women, either as a solo concert, by groups, or in ballets as a choreographic style. A brilliant, vigorous, technically demanding dance; continuous whirling pivots are a highlight. New ballets produced by Bharatiya Kala Kendra (Indian Art Association) in New Delhi are in Kathak style.

Western modern drama reached India in the late seventeen hundreds via amateur English theatricals performed by resident British businessmen, civil servants, and their wives. Professional troupes followed. Tagore applied the Western form of spoken drama to Indian subjects, writing in both English and Bengali. Banal, commercial drama in the Western mold, has been around for a hundred years. In the past two decades the modern-drama scene has come to life; talented young playwrights are writing of the search for a modern Indian identity in contemporary society. The plays of Girish Karnad, Badal Sarkar, Mohan Rakesh, and Tendulkar are exciting works; they are being translated and performed in various regional languages through India. Not since Sanskrit times has there been pan-Indian drama. Modern drama troupes of long standing exist; most are amateur, some are semiprofessional; the best are very good and worth seeing.

WHERE TO GO

NEW DELHI. Capital of India and theater center of Hindi-speaking north India. A government city, built in the 1930s, without strong dramatic traditions of its own, it is a convenient place to see visiting dance and drama troupes from other parts of the country. One or two productions a week, as a rule; modern drama, two to four performances, and other types, a single performance only. New Delhi theaters are easy to get to and comfortable; there aren't many and they are mediocre in quality, however. The daily *Statesman* and weekly *Delhi Diary* carry good theater listings; on pillars of Connaught Place look for posters; play handbills are in some hotel lobbies; you can buy tickets conveniently at Central Cottage Emporium on Janpath Road. Special theater festivals are always worth attending. Commemorating Republic Day, tribal groups from remote districts present massive programs of folk dances at National Stadium on January 26 and 27. Outstanding artists of modern and traditional drama are invited to perform as part of Akademi Awards Ceremony Arts Festival, at Rabindra Bhavan, the last week in February. Most winters there is a nightly Sound and Light Show at Red Fort in Old Delhi; during the day from the river bank, below the fort walls, snake charmers, trained bears, and—believe it or not—levitators vie for your attention and tossed coins. Except during the summer, good, inexpensive classical dance performances are arranged for tourists at the YWCA and YMCA (both on Jai Singh Road).

All India Fine Arts and Crafts Society (AIFACS) **Hall****. One of the busiest halls in New Delhi. Rents to amateur drama and music groups; also classical dance and traditional drama perform here. An intimate proscenium theater, small, and lacking facilities. Older building; comfortable; seats 500; moderately comfortable. English-language programs.

Ferozeshah Kotla Grounds***. Huge (3,000 seat) open-air theater for large-scale ballet. All seats reserved; bring binoculars if you aren't in first class. Two week runs of Krishna Lila Ballet, August–September, and Ram Lila Ballet, September–October, are major yearly events in New Delhi. Massive casts move across wide center stage and adjoining side stages; superb costuming; dance style is blend of several classical and regional dances (this upsets purists but need not bother us).

Kamani Auditorium ***. Spartan in design, built in 1970, the city's best and most comfortable theater. Seats 900 in well-raked orchestra; pushback, plush seats; air-conditioned; all reserved seats; coffee bar. Owned by Bharatiya Kala Kendra arts association and school; once or twice monthly bills of classical dance concerts, song recitals, and ballet performances by excellent artists are highly recommended. Also rents to other groups. Threenight festival of folk arts, including dance and music, in adjoining courtyard on the weekend before Holi is great fun, a carnival for kids and grownups.

National School of Drama Outdoor Theater **. In a beautiful setting; a small open stage nestles under the trees. Sit under the stars on rugs spread on the grass and on steps of the intimate semicircular amphitheater (300 seats). Major productions of the school, and of especially invited regional troupes which are sponsored by the Sangeet Natak Akademi, play here. Highly recommended. No reserved seating; often free admission; English program; coffee bar behind amphitheater.

Rabindra Bhavan (Tagore House)**. Home of the Sangeet Natak Akademi (Akademi of Music, Dance, and Drama), and constituent National School of Drama, and Art Gallery. Exhibits of theatrical masks and performance photographs in lobbies; excellent theater library; no theater in the building. Often festivals of shadow-plays, dance-plays, balladeering, and other regional forms given in *shamiyana* tent set up on adjacent lawn can save you a thousand-mile trip to the boondocks. Don't miss it; normally free; ask for invitation card at desk; no reserved seating; tent can seat 1,200, so come early for folding chair up front. I prefer sprawling on a rug in front of the stage myself. In Delhi's cold morning air you will want a coat or blanket.

Sapru House**. A utilitarian concert hall that is often used as a theater. Small stage is without stage equipment. Seats 600 on single-level, slightly raked orchestra; plastic-covered seats; overhead fans. A rental house for modern-drama and occasional classical-dance concerts.

Triveni Garden Theater**. A tiny, intimate outdoor amphitheater; seats a mere 200 on its semicircular raised steps. A charmer, but rarely used. Art gallery and snack bar adjoining. A nice place to relax for a few minutes at lunch or in the afternoon.

BOMBAY. India's major port, a merchant's city. Theater in Bombay is like the city itself: highly commercial, well organized, Western in outlook, and not especially unique, nor particularly "Indian." In a week you can see up to 20 plays. Among Bombay's dozen theaters one alone has adequate equipment and stage facilities; many are concert halls. Some theaters are open nightly; to accommodate Bombay's millions of commuters three performances are squeezed into each weekend day (morning, matinee, and evening shows). Unlike the rest of India where people stay home during the heavy summer rains, this is a time when theaters in Bombay are jammed to the rafters with spectators. Movies captured part of the live theater audience right after World War II; now the situation is reversed and live drama plays to huge audiences. Theater ads appear daily in the *Times of India* (see the Wednesday edition especially). Vernacular papers carry complete listings— informative if you can get someone to translate for you. Weekly tourist magazines tell you almost nothing. Theaters are scattered over a very large area; except for a few theaters in the center of town, you will have to travel by taxi or city bus.

There are two language communities—Marathi and Gujerati—and two distinct theater establishments in Bombay. Marathi professional theater†† is big business. Troupes tour out of Bombay, some in their own luxury buses, to 300 towns in Maharashtra State. "Pathos and laughter" formula plays draw huge and enthusiastic middle-class audiences; applause bursts forth every few minutes; noisy children are indignantly hushed. The plays are blatant and banal but you may appreciate the superlative acting craftsmanship of Dr. Lagu, star of the Goa Hindu Association troupe, or Bal Kolhatakar's touching Chaplinesque roles with the Durwanchi Judi troupe. Other major troupes: Natya Sampada, Chandra Leka, Natya Mandir. Interesting productions of serious modern scripts are staged, usually on weekends, by excellent Marathi amateur groups: Rangayan, Theater Unit, Avishkar. (Theaters: Ravindra Natya Mandir, Shivaji Natya Mandir.)

Good Gujerati modern drama†† is produced by the Indian National Theater (INT) and Prasthan. INT also has a ballet division. Several workers' drama groups do ideological plays among Gujerati laborers. The typical Gujerati audience member, it is said, is a storekeeper who cannot close his doors during the week, explaining why Gujerati plays run weekends only, and why the typical play is an innocuous little domestic comedy. There are many troupes.

Watch out for Adi Marzban's slick versions of recent Broadway comedies aimed at Bombay's large Parsee (Zoroastrian Persian) community; moderately well done, you can't tell the play by its Indian title and who wants to hear Neil Simon jokes in Gujerati? (Theaters: Birla Matushri Sabhagar, Jai Hind Auditorium, Patkar Hall, Bhulabhai Desai Auditorium.) If you have a taste for theater slumming, see the Deshi Natak Samaj troupe belt out old-style musical melodramas (theater: Bhang Wedi) or, if it is in town, see the Usha Troupe. Tamasha can be seen nightly (theater: New Hanuman). A State Tamasha Festival, held in November or December, rotates yearly among the cities of Bombay, Poona, Aurangabad, and Sangli. (For information write the Chief Officer for Cultural Activities and Secretary Recreation Committee, Old Secretariat Building, Bombay 1.) Bombay has no hotel or tourist shows of interest. Musical shows featuring "playback artists," that is, movie dub-in singers, are popular and eminently missable.

Bhang Wedi (Princess or Old Princess Theater)**. A remarkable Victorian relic with original cast-iron grillwork outside, musicians' "cage," six-foot high stage, and intimate curving balcony that starts at second row of orchestra. Seats 500 in orchestra and 200 in balcony; clean; sedate atmosphere; fairly comfortable seats; many fans, cool; nightly performance and weekend matinees; snacks sold outside during intermission. Play synopsis, in Gujerati, sells for a few pennies. Home theater of Deshi Natak Samaj (National Drama Group) of nineteenth-century melodrama tradition. Fantastic, steel-lunged elocution; words seem to hang suspended in the air; attractive actresses; prompting from the wings; electric bell signals stage drops to rise and fall. Magical caves, abductions, missing jewels, battles, ribald interludes, and songs one after the other. An incredible experience, like stepping back 80 years into a vanished era.

Bharatiya Vidya Bhavan (India House of Learning)**. A functional, clean, but unexciting hall; institutional atmosphere. Seats 500 in wide, shallow orchestra and 200 in poor, far-back balcony; hard seats; air-conditioned; all reserved seats. Rents to various groups, mostly schools.

Bhulabhai Desai Auditorium ***. Modern; comfortable; air-conditioned; 900 plush seats in orchestra and large balcony. A rental theater.

Birla Matushri Sabhagar (Birla Hall)***. A concert hall with poor stage facilities but an elegant and spacious interior. Seats 1,160 on concave orchestra level; very comfortable; air-conditioned; can reserve a seat by phone. Rents mostly to amateur troupes and school societies.

Jai Hind Auditorium **. Small (seats 580) and cozy; narrow orchestra; comfortable push-back seats; air-conditioned; all reserved seating. A pleasant house and popular with modern-drama groups. Stage is a mere 25 feet wide. Rents to any group.

National Centre for the Performing Arts*. A tiny jewel of a music hall; wood paneled, intimate; sophisticated decor; seats 100; air-conditioned. Small stage is good only for music, solo dance concerts, poetry reading, and experimental one-act plays. The Centre plans to build two new theaters and a concert hall next to the Sheraton-Oberoi Hotel on the bay.

New Hanuman*. A grimy shed-theater for workers; in the middle of the industrial section of town; not for the fastidious. Seats 400 on orchestra level; old cushioned chairs and benches; overhead fans. This is the main Tamasha house in Bombay and home of comic actor Dadu. Bill changes nightly. Audience offers money to actresses to sing favorite Tamasha songs. Can reserve seat by phone; manager speaks excellent English.

Patkar Hall*. Poor stage facilities; comfortable auditorium; spacious feeling; seats 750 in gently sloping orchestra; soft seats; air-conditioned. Often rented for Gujerati comedies and amateur English-language plays.

Rang Bhavan (Building of Colors)***. An outdoor amphitheater; seats 3,000 on folding metal chairs; bring your own cushion; sit close to see well. An important rental theater for large, commercial productions. You can often see spectacular historical plays here.

Ravindra Natya Mandir ***. A "Tagore Theater," owned by Maharashtra State. One of the better theaters in Bombay and much in demand for semiprofessional and professional plays, music, and dance recitals. Rented out almost every day. Well-equipped stage; seats 800 in warm, carpeted orchestra and small balcony; push-back, soft seats; air-conditioned; all seating reserved; soft drink and snack bar.

Shanmukhananda Hall*. A huge theater; quite far from the center of town; used for popular music and dance programs more than for legitimate drama. Seats 3,000 in orchestra and two large balconies; air-conditioned; comfortable, all reserved seating; can book by phone. Often exceptionally expensive tickets. Moderately large stage (50 feet) with curved forestage.

Shivaji Natya Mandir (also **Shivaji Mandir**, **Shivaji Hall**)***. New, utilitarian theater; seats 1,000 in orchestra and one large balcony; seats tilt forward uncomfortably; air-conditioned. More heavily used than any other Bombay theater; 15–16 performances a week. In a very busy part of town; almost always crowded; play scripts sold in house, snacks in foyer.

Tejpal Auditorium*. A handsome, new performance hall; suited to small plays and dance recitals. Not used by major groups. Seats 600 in small, broad, and shallow orchestra; soft, push-back seats; air-conditioned.

CALCUTTA. India's most exciting theater city. Poverty and crowding do not make Calcutta every visitor's dream destination, but the theater here is vitally alive. Calcutta's actors and actresses are mobile of gesture and facile in elocution. Bengali is a liquid, expressive language. Every Bengali is a performer, they say; but not every Bengali is a director. In Calcutta you go to see the star performer, not carefully wrought ensemble acting.

A well-educated, sophisticated, elite audience supports classical dance concerts and music recitals. (Theaters: Kala Mandir and Rabindra Sadan.) The two-week Banga Sanskriti Festival in June is devoted to programs of classical music, dance, and sometimes Sanskrit play productions (for information write Banga Sanskriti Sammelan, Marcus Square, Calcutta). Modern drama is Calcutta's pride. From the time of Rabindranath Tagore, new, experimental drama has flourished here. Two troupes are outstanding today. Bohurupee is led by husband and wife, Sombhu and Tripti Mitra, regarded by many as the country's two most gifted performers. Nandikar specializes in adaptations of serious Western drama; Ajitesh Bannerjee is its leading actor and director.

Jatra is seen irregularly in Calcutta; winter is the best time to look for street performances. Actor-director Utpal Dutt has created "modern Jatra," applying Jatra techniques to modern themes; his People's Little Theater is strongly political. Communist and workers' drama is regularly staged, sometimes amateurishly (at Mukta Angan), sometimes with great skill and effect (at Minerva Theater).

The flourishing Bengali commercial drama is so bad you don't know whether to laugh or cry when faced with what a Calcutta critic calls its "coarse entertainment, cheap sentimentality, and extravagant melodrama." Plots are stolen from third-rate novels; talentless movie stars posture and pose; there is absolutely no stage direction at all; theater surroundings are dismal. Remember where such theatrical travesties are staged (theaters: Star, Biswaroopa, Rung Mahal) and you can avoid them. But just in case you should go, out of curiosity, sit eight to ten rows back from the high stages for good viewing.

Calcutta has 20–30 productions a week. Theaters cluster in two areas: old, run-down commercial theaters in "old Calcutta" about a mile north of the Maidan downtown; and modern concert halls and auditoriums south of the Maidan, in the area of the Victoria Memorial. A few theaters are in other parts of the city. Thursday, Saturday, and Sunday are usual performance nights, plus weekend matinees; other nights theaters are dark or rent to minor groups. Very complete play listings appear in the *Sunday Statesman*, the Tourist Bureau's *Calcutta This Fortnight*, and biweekly *What's on in Calcutta*. Commercial troupes advertise in daily English-language *Amrita Bazar Patrika*. Taxis are plentiful and cheap. Streetcars run north and south and stop near most theaters and can be fun if you have time and aren't bothered by crowds. Calcutta is a live-in city, densely crowded, the streets thronged with moving crowds day and night.

Academy of Fine Arts**. The main building contains a moderate-sized auditorium; pleasant atmosphere; fairly comfortable seats on orchestra level. Rents primarily for classical-music concerts and dance recitals.

Biswaroopa*. An old Victorian-style theater; ancient and decrepit, but revolving stage still works. Seats 700 on hard chairs; overhead fans; all seats reserved. Permanent home of dreadful Biswaroopa commercial troupe; B-movie material; organ and violin in the background; much weeping and wailing; lower middle-class audience.

Kala Mandir (Palace of Arts)*******. Best modern auditorium in Calcutta. Wide stage and fairly good equipment; seats 1,100 in orchestra and balcony; spacious lobby; tasteful decor; comfortable seating; air-conditioned; snacks on balcony roof during intermission. A rental house; many important festivals use this hall; elite audience.

Minerva Theater*. Another holdover from the Victorian era. At one time must have been stunning, with two small horseshoe-shaped balconies; now dilapidated and only some 400 seats in orchestra can be used. It is, however, clean; hard narrow seats; overhead fans. Usual play run is several months. Home of permanent troupe of full-time laborers and intellectuals who perform didactic Marxist plays; intense, disciplined acting; declamatory and narrative production style influenced by Brecht; fluid lighting; imaginative and strong staging; worth seeing. Not advertised in newspapers; look for listing in *Calcutta This Fortnight*. Usually SRO weekends; half-empty Thursdays.

Mukta Angan (Free Theater)*****. A corrugated-metal roofed shed; cement floor; 450 folding metal chairs; primitive stage; all reserved seats; overhead fans. A genuine youth and workers' theater; in working-class district; audience heckles and drowns out performers if they don't like something. A rental theater; usually a single performance by young, small, inexperienced groups; modern, experimental plays; tickets are cheap.

Rabindra Sadan (Tagore House)*******. A pleasant, new, 1,100-seat concert hall; modern design; air-conditioned; comfortable; conveniently located by Victoria Memorial. Rents to any group; often classical-dance and music recitals.

Rangana (Playhouse)******. An older theater in good repair. Seats 800 in orchestra and balcony; seats are fairly comfortable; overhead fans; all seats reserved; snack vendors come through the house during intermission. Theater is leased Thursday, Saturday, and Sunday to excellent Nandikar troupe; usually sold out; very popular. Other nights theater is dark or rents to other groups.

Rung Mahal *. Another old commercial theater; falling down. Same kind of awful play you can see in better surroundings at Star.

Star* **. Best of the commercial theater buildings in Calcutta; old but clean; pleasant interior; air-conditioned; seats 900 in orchestra and balcony; moderately comfortable; all seats reserved; English program costs a quarter of a rupee. Home of permanent commercial stock company; marvelously bad acting bits—head tossing, eye wiping, throat clearing, handkerchief flicking, posing in meaningless clichés; stock scenery moves on small revolving stage; middle-class audiences keep a play running three to four years here. If you *must* see one of Calcutta's dreadful commercial melodramas, at least you will be comfortable at Star.

Theatre Centre **. Seats 100 on hard chairs set before a tiny stage; overhead fans. A laboratory theater; set up by husband-and-wife team, Tarun and Dipanwita Roy. Each Sunday they perform in Broadway-style modern comedies and character studies. Rents to small, young, often avant-garde, groups other nights. The theater is an adjunct of the Theatre Centre Drama School. All seats reserved (but room is so small it doesn't matter where you sit); English program; coffee during intermission.

MADRAS. Capital of Tamil Nadu State. The citadel of southern, or Karnatic, tradition in music and dance. The devotion of the Tamils to performing arts is seen in the unique system of community *sabhas*, local cultural organizations, that are the chief sponsors of music, dance, and drama in Madras. Many sabhas have their own halls, contributing to the large number of auditoriums in the city. Since a sabha serves a particular region of the city, halls are scattered; there is no central theater district. For an annual subscription fee, a sabha member can go to two or three cultural events a month. People gather from all parts of India to attend the famous Christmas festival sponsored by Madras' major sabhas. The excitement then is palpable.

For two weeks (from about December 20 until January 2), the Music Academy, Indian Fine Arts Society, Mylapore Fine Arts Club, Brahma Gana Sabha, Sri Krishna Gana Sabha, and other sabhas bring India's finest traditional musicians, singers, dancers, and theater groups to perform. Going nonstop, you can only sample from each day's 15–20 concerts, recitals, stage productions, lectures, and demonstrations that run from morning into the night. Excellent and unusual dance-dramas are specially staged. The festival is a must if you are traveling in India during Christmas; tickets to sabha events are sold to the general public. April–June, months that are blast-furnace hot, mark the low point of the Madras theater season.

Modern drama in Madras is pretty tame stuff. There are no exciting experiments going on. Most productions are fluff performed by amateurs, and the sabha system virtually guarantees a dozen paid performances for even the most mediocre and insipid production. Don't be fooled by English play titles; English is widely spoken in Madras and playwrights are fond of putting English titles to Tamil language plays. Your eyes aren't deceiving you if you notice the same scenery and furniture in different theaters on consecutive nights; modern-drama groups don't bother to design and construct scenery suited to the play—they rent stock pieces from commercial scenic firms. It is something of a mystery why an otherwise highly literate and sophisticated Tamil audience puts up with this foolish kind of theater.

Until a decade ago, a number of highly successful professional companies toured the state doing old-fashioned, bombastic musical dramas. Current productions of two-star actors are offshoots of this tradition. R. S. Manohar has built up a tremendous following for his National Theatı lavishly costumed, elaborately staged legendary and historical dramas. Manohar is a straightforward, powerful actor of the old school. "Major" Sundararajan and his Ennessen Theatres troupe perform sentimental melodramas. Plays are set in the present but performance style is out of the dim past.

The logistics of theatergoing is simple in Madras. It is a small city and distances to theaters are not great; taxis are easy to find and cheap; theater locations are clearly shown on the excellent *Guide to Madras* city map (Maps and Atlases Publications, Ltd.); complete daily theater listings appear in the English-language *Hindu*; theater programs are almost always printed in English. On the first of each month sabhas advertise their monthly cultural schedule in the *Hindu*. Tickets are more expensive in Madras than in other Indian cities.

Kalakshetra (Holy Place of Arts) **Auditorium** ****. Set in the quiet countryside a few miles south of Madras city. A beautiful, natural wood structure constructed as an open-sided, high-roofed pavilion; an unusually warm, relaxed atmosphere. Well-designed, 60-foot open stage without proscenium; ideal for dance-dramas, a Kalakshetra specialty. Seats 500; comfortable wicker basket-chairs in first class; hard folding-metal chairs at the back for unreserved seating; best seats are row C center. Good seats are quickly sold; order in advance by phone. No photos; no recordings; remove shoes at the door; English program; refreshments on the lawn. This is the auditorium of Rukmini Devi's internationally known Kalakshetra school for the arts, established in 1936. Six or more newly choreographed dance-plays are developed each year in various classical styles; usually shown in public, one performance only of each play, during the Christmas festival.

Museum Theater***. Unusual antiquarian indoor amphitheater with high-domed ceiling, yet small enough that all seats are close. Delightful. Seats 450 on cane-bottomed chairs; any seat on the semicircular stepped area is good; orchestra seats in the center are the poorest. An older building; part of Madras Museum; well maintained; overhead fans. Theater is rented to small amateur groups; young, elite audience.

Music Academy Hall***. Best and most modern auditorium in Madras. Seats 1,100 in broad, shallow orchestra and high balcony; comfortable cushioned seats; air-conditioned; snacks served outside during intermission; stage moderately well equipped. Auditorium of the Music Academy of Madras, the city's oldest and most important sabha. Its two-week Christmas festival bill includes morning lectures and demonstrations, two music sessions each afternoon, and two major music, dance, or dance-drama performances each evening. All seats reserved, and single tickets much in demand. Festival program is available in English.

Mylapore Fine Arts Club**. A drab, rectangular shed with walls of woven palm leaves; in a good residential district. Seats 900; first class in comfortable wicker basket-chairs; slightly raked concrete floor; overhead fans; all seats reserved. Audience mostly middle class.

N.K.T. Kalamantap (N.K.T. Arts Pavilion)***. An outdoor theater, seating 2,500; in spacious, pleasant grounds of girls' school. Often packed for ponderous historical plays. Comfortable wicker basket-chairs in first class; concrete benches at the rear; proscenium stage is huge; wide pit pushes stage far from even front row of seats; sit close or bring binoculars; snacks are sold by vendors during intermission.

Rajah Annamalai Hall***. Second best theater in the city; fine size for seeing and hearing (890 seats); well-raked orchestra; no balcony; soft seats; air-conditioned. Spacious feeling from marble side porticos. Owning cultural organization, Tamil Isai Sangham, sponsors own performances and rents to various groups.

Rama Rau Kala Mantapa (Rama Rau Arts Pavilion)**. A small, utilitarian, undistinguished rectangular hall; seats 600 on slightly raked orchestra; no air-conditioning. Rents to various groups.

Rasika Ranjani Sabha Hall **. Another utilitarian hall; seats 700 on steeply raked orchestra; big, deep, sleep-engendering wicker basket-chairs in first class; an old building; overhead fans, but still hot and stuffy when crowded; no printed program. The sabha sponsors its own performances and rents to other groups.

South India Athletic Association (SIAA) **Grounds** *. Grubby, temporary little theaters set up at the end of the racetrack for a few weeks. Usually 400–600 folding chairs under a roof of bamboo fronds tied to a network of poles. This is where the few remaining old-style sung-drama troupes play in Madras. A good time to find a troupe is December 28, night of fasting (Vaikunta Ekadasi), when people see a play in order to stay awake through the night.

Sri Krishna Gana Sabha (Sri Krishna Singing Society)*. A very unattractive shed building; dirt floor; walls of woven palm leaves; inconveniently far out in the suburbs. A cavernous place (seats 1,200); comfortable first-class wicker basket-chairs; circulating fans; all seats reserved; snacks during intermission. The sabha sponsors performances and rents to other groups occasionally.

University Centenary Auditorium***. Largest theater in India; seats 3,260; built in 1965; spartan interior; extremely comfortable push-back seats; air-conditioned. Owned by University of Madras; rents to student and other performing groups. Stage is 60 feet wide; deep forestage as well; good for music and dance programs; too large for drama. Used less often than other auditoriums.

Vani Mahal (Palace of Goddess of Learning)**. A shed theater open on the sides; an old building. Seats 800 on almost flat concrete floor; first-class wicker chairs are fairly comfortable; circulating fans; English-language program; snacks served during intermission. Often used for Indian Fine Arts Society performances.

REGIONAL PERFORMANCES

Visitors are welcome at most regional performances in India. A few of the more important and dependable festivals are described here; there are many more. Dates can change from year to year. For more specific information write to the festival or performance group at the local addresses given below.

AHMEDABAD, GUJERAT STATE. Private Darpana music and dance school organizes five-day Darpana Dance Festival, first week in October. Kuchipudi, Kathakali, Bharata Natyam, shadow-plays and other performances. (Darpana, Chidambaram, Ahmedabad 13, Gujerat)

CHERUTHURUTHY, KERALA STATE. March 14th and 15th, Kerala Kalamandalam Dance Festival celebrates the anniversary of the founding of the Kerala Kalamandalam (Kerala Drama Academy). There are Kathakali and sometimes Kudiyattam performances at the school's new buildings. Superb performances. North of Cochin 4 hours by rented car or 8–10 hours by bus or train.

GURUVAYUR, KERALA STATE. Beginning on Dusshera day, September–October, the eight-night Krishnattam Dance Festival is held in the Guruvayur Temple. May not be open to outsiders. Inquire. (Guruvayur Temple Managing Committee, Guruvayur, Ernakulam, Kerala)

HYDERABAD, ANDHRA PRADESH STATE. The Andhra Pradesh Akademi organizes the Akademi Music, Dance, and Drama Festival, November 1–5. Modern and classical theater are both included. Held in Ravindra Bharathi Building, Saifabad, Hyderabad 4.

JAMMU and *SRINAGAR, JAMMU/KASHMIR STATE.* The Jammu/Kashmir Akademi organizes the Akademi Music Festival twice yearly: at the city of Jammu in March and at the city of Srinagar in September. This festival features athletic north-Indian dancing. (Jammu and Kashmir Academy of Art, Culture, and Language, Lalmandi, Srinagar, or 40 Exchange Road, Jammu)

KUCHIPUDI VILLAGE, ANDHRA PRADESH STATE. To see genuine Kuchipudi dance-drama (not just dance excerpts) you need to travel to the village home of the art. The Shri Siddhendra Kalakshetram (Siddhendra School of Kuchipudi) is the chief Kuchipudi training school in India. It sponsors a three-day Kuchipudi Dance Festival each year in August–September, at the time of Krishna's birthday (Janmashtami). Major Kuchipudi plays are performed by the best professional artists. You can fly from Hyderabad to Vijayawara and then take a hired car two hours to Kuchipudi Village. Or go eight hours by express train from Hyderabad to Vijayawara (stop at Warangal one way, hire a car, and see beautiful statues of dancers at nearby Ramappa Temple at Palampet).

KULU, HIMACHAL PRADESH STATE. Dussera is celebrated with five nights of processions of village gods, rituals, and dances at government-organized Kulu Dusshera Festival. Some performances in outdoor theater, with towering Himalaya Mountains as a backdrop. Kulu is a remote hill town, 250 miles north of New Delhi, that can be reached only by car or bus. (Dusserha Committee, Kulu, Himachal Pradesh)

MELATUR VILLAGE, TANJORE (THANJAVUR), TAMIL NADU STATE. The original village where male dance-plays in Bharata Natyam style, Bhagavatha Mela, are performed as religious offerings. Bhagavatha Mela Festival continues for over a week during the first part of May; main plays in the repertory are performed by local village actors in simple surroundings. A long 240 miles south of Madras at a time of dreadful heat, this trip is only for the hardy.

PATNA, BIHAR STATE.   A festival of Manipuri, Bharata Natyam, and Kathakali classical dancing is organized the third week in September by the Bharatiya Nritya Kala Mandir (Indian Dramatic Dance Association).

SERAIKELLA VILLAGE, BIHAR STATE.   A sophisticated and delicate masked dance, *Chhau*†††, has long been supported by ruling families of the district. Several troupes perform Chhau dances in the Royal Palace courtyard for two or three days, on the occasion of the Sun Festival, falling on the last day of the Bengali New Year, April 13. Seraikella is about 150 miles west of Calcutta, a few miles from Sindri rail junction. (Srikalapitha, the Palace, Seraikella, Bihar, or Government Chhau Dance Training Centre, Seraikella, Bihar.) On the same days, Chhau dances also can be seen at Chhau Dance Festival, Purulia, West Bengal State; and Chhau Dance Festival, Baripada, Orissa State. The former is about 50 miles northeast and the latter 75 miles southeast of Seraikella.

TRIVANDRUM, KERALA STATE.   As part of Shri Padmanabhaswamy Temple celebrations, Kathakali troupes from around the state gather to perform at Kathakali Dance Festival twice a year: in the month of Meenam, March–April, and the month of Thulam, October–November. A major Kathakali event. (For information write Kerala Sangeetha Nataka Akademi, Trichur 1, Kerala.)

UDIPI TOWN, MYSORE STATE.   The State Akademi Yakshagana Festival is held for five days the first week in November in this small, isolated, difficult-to-get-to town on the Arabian Sea. Important Yakshagama troupes from around the state gather here to perform. (For information write Mysore State Sangeetha Nataka Academy, Ravindra Kalakshetra, Bangalore 2, Mysore.)

Books to Read

GENERAL: Balwant Gargi, *Theatre in India* (New York: Theatre Arts Books, 1962), and *Folk Theatre in India* (Seattle, Wash.: University of Washington Press, 1966); Clifford R. and Betty True Jones, *Kathakali* (San Francisco and New York: American Society for Eastern Arts, 1970); A. B. Keith, *The Sanskrit Drama* (London: Oxford University Press, 1970); Kapila Vatsyayan, *Classical Indian Dance in Literature and the Arts* (New Delhi: Sangeet Natak Akademi, 1968).

PLAYS: J. A. B. van Buitenen, *Two Plays of Ancient India* (New York: Columbia University Press, 1968); Kalidasa, *Shakuntala and Other Writings* (New York: Dutton, 1969); P. Lal, *Great Sanskrit Plays* (New York: New Directions, 1957); Rabindranath Tagore, *Sacrifice and Other Plays* (New York: Macmillan, 1917); Henry W. Wells, *Sanskrit Plays from Epic Sources* (Baroda: University of Baroda, 1968).

Indonesia

I t is easy to feel a special fondness for Indonesia. It is one of the most beautiful island chains on earth. Its people are gentle and kind. Its plays and dances are beguiling in their warmth and grace; many are of the highest quality. In number and variety of dramatic forms few countries surpass Indonesia. There are shadow-plays, puppet-plays, classical dance-dramas, and ritual theater; there is popular drama in a variety of guises; there is modern and avant-garde drama.

You will want time in Indonesia. A two- or three-day visit that makes sense in other places is madness here. Indonesia is too big; there is too much to do. You will find your truly great theatrical experiences after you leave Djakarta, the national capital, and travel into the provinces—to Bandung in West Java, to Jogjakarta and Surakarta in Central Java, and on to the island of Bali. I think two weeks is minimum; stay longer if you can. You won't regret it. If time is no object, there are also a multitude of folk and religious ritual dances performed on Sumatra, Kalimantan (Borneo), Sulawesi, Halmahera, Ambon, Banda, West Irian (New Guinea), Flores, Timor, Sumba, Sumbawa, and other islands; all are accessible, though they are remote and rarely ever visited by tourists.

THEATERGOING

Commercial theaters operate nightly through the year. Professional dance-drama and popular historical-drama troupes are permanent organizations that will stay at a theater as long as it is profitable, for several months or for years. A theater bill begins at 8:00 P.M. and lasts for three or four hours. A preliminary dance scene may precede the main play. A different play is performed (in part ad libbed) each night. Audience reaction can be lively: shouts to the actors, requests for songs, money thrown on the stage. Vendors move through the aisles selling peanuts, coffee, ice cream. Seats are reserved in even the most humble theater. To be sure of a good seat at a good theater buy your tickets in the afternoon. First-class tickets, except for special tourist performances, are inexpensive. Foreign spectators are still a rarity, and at most theaters you will be given the best seats without asking. Puppet plays last all night, about nine hours. If you cannot stay the whole time, don't miss the midnight to 2:00 A.M. clown scenes. Puppet performances are rarely in commercial theaters; they are commissioned for a single night and admission is not charged. They can be exasperatingly hard to find, but you will be welcome if you manage to stumble across one.

THEATER BUILDINGS. There are probably 150 commercial theater buildings in Java; you will find one in most medium-sized towns, more in cities. Unfortunately, you will also find them hot, unventilated, dirty, miserable places with few exceptions. Temporary theaters made of a bamboo framework covered with palm thatch are common in smaller towns. The better and more accessible theaters are mentioned here. Shadow-plays, puppet-plays, and performances in Bali take place out-of-doors, before a temple, in a dance pavilion, or in the shelter of the open vestibule of an ordinary home. Seating may be on folding chairs or on mats spread on the ground.

SEASON. Indonesia has a marked wet and dry season, corresponding respectively to our winter and summer. The ideal time to visit is during the hot, dry summer months, June–September. Sporadic but torrential rains make November–March a poorer time to come because there are fewer outdoor performances. Rain does not stop performances in Bali; when the shower passes, the play goes on.

FESTIVALS. The majority of Indonesians are Moslem; religious holidays are not important occasions for theater performances. Plays and dances are performed on outdoor stages set up in town squares in celebration of Hari Merdeka, Independence Day, August 17. Two spectacular dance festivals are held in Java for tourists, Indonesian and foreign, during the summer months on nights of the full moon. Oldest and best known is the Ramayana Ballet that runs four consecutive nights each month before the Loro Djonggrang Temple at Prambanan, near Jogjakarta in Central Java, May through October. More recently established, the Tjandrawilwatikta Dance Festival, at an amphitheater set in the mountains near Tretes, East Java, runs two consecutive nights a month during the full-moon, May through October.

In Hindu Bali, religious festivals are the occasions for thousands of the finest performances of plays and dances through the year. Because each Balinese village has several temples and each temple has an annual festival, Odalan, festival performances are happening, somewhere on Bali, virtually every day of the year. Especially important for theater are the ten days of the Balinese New Year—the days between Galungan and Kuningan—and the day or two following. A half-dozen performances can be seen each day. The New Year occurs every 210 days, or: November 12–22, 1975; June 9–19, 1976; January 5–15, 1977; August 3–13, 1977; March 1–11, 1978; September 27–October 7, 1978; April 25–May 5, 1979; November 21–December 1, 1979; June 18–28, 1980; January 14–24, 1981; August 12–22, 1981; March 10–20, 1982; October 6–16, 1982; May 4–14, 1983; November 30–December 10, 1983; June 27–July 7, 1984; January 23–February 2, 1985; August 21–31, 1985 and so on. If it is possible to arrange to be in Bali one of these times, by all means do so; you will be in for the time of your life.

TRANSPORTATION. Djakarta and Den Pasar, Bali, are international airports. Indonesia is not on the main east-west Asian air route, however, a fact that accounts for the relatively small number of tourists visiting the islands. Of course the quickest way to travel within Indonesia is by air. A fairly good air-conditioned daily express train connects Djakarta, Jogjakarta, Surakarta, and Surabaya on Java. The trip takes about 18 hours. If you are hardy and can brave the heat of a nonair-conditioned coach, it is a beautiful but slow two-day trip by local train from Djakarta through the mountains to Bandung and from there to Jogjakarta. Nothing, however, matches driving from Djakarta, past smoking volcanoes and verdant scenery, the length of Java to the east coast, and there putting your car on the ferry to Bali. The road goes through rain-forested mountains and lush rice fields. It is a magnificent way to combine sightseeing and theatergoing. Cars can be rented in Djakarta; the trip takes four or five days minimum.

Public transportation in cities is not very satisfactory. Taxis do not cruise. I suggest you use, in order of decreasing convenience and expense: unmetered taxis ordered by the hour or the day from your hotel; in Djakarta three-wheeled metered scooter-cabs, called *helitjaks*, whose drivers will not know English; and *betjaks*, man-powered trishaws. Betjaks are everywhere and for short trips they are the common form of city transportation; set the price with the driver before you start. In Bali there are no betjaks. Motorbikes and motorcycles can be rented cheaply by the day or week (Sanur hotel area or in downtown Den Pasar); or bargain for a small panel truck, called *bemo*, that rents, driver and all, for perhaps ten dollars a day (one-half to one-third the cost of a taxi). In some cities you can take a *dokar*, or horse cart, costing about the same as a betjak.

INFORMATION.   Published information is scarce in Indonesia. English-language newspapers list or advertise a few Djakarta events. The Directorate General of Tourism, Djakarta, publishes annually *Indonesia: Important Events*; you may be able to get a free copy from an Indonesian Consulate. When you arrive in Djakarta, be sure to pick up a copy of the Taman Ismail Marzuki (Djakarta Arts Center) monthly *Calendar of Events*; it lists (in English) all productions scheduled for its five theaters. *Welcome to Jogjakarta*, by the Jogjakarta Tourist Promotion Board, is helpful; free at your hotel.

WHAT TO SEE

Wayang Kulit shadow-drama†††† is the most ancient and revered dramatic form in Indonesia. Through tropical evenings, mythological heroes and heroines—borrowed from the *Mahabharata*, to a lesser extent from the *Ramayana* (see **India**), and from other legendary sources—have played out their heroic dramas before the Wayang Kulit screen for at least a thousand years, and probably more. Elegant Prince Ardjuna, lover of a hundred thousand women and implacable warrior, is the major hero; he and the other Pandawa brothers appear in play after play. Three (sometimes four) low-comedy clowns accompany the Pandawas; descended from the gods, they mix sage advice with buffoonery. Crude ogres roar and hurl themselves across the screen. Exciting, intricately executed battle scenes bring the audience to life again and again in the course of the night-long performance.

Wayang Kulit is a one-man show: one puppeteer manipulates exquisitely carved leather puppets, speaks the dialogue of each character, chants narration, and sings mood songs. He doesn't move from his sitting position before the white cloth screen for nine hours, until the play finishes with the coming of dawn. Lovely, sonorous, endlessly moving music of a gamelan ensemble's bronze instruments underscores changing emotions; 150 melodies and songs match every conceivable dramatic circumstance. There are many shadow-theaters in Asia (India, Thailand, Cambodia, Malaysia, China) but none is as artistically subtle and spiritually moving as Javanese Wayang Kulit. The number of professional puppeteers amounts to thousands. A performance is a consecrated event, commissioned in honor of marriage, birth, circumcision, or other auspicious event; the stage is the veranda of the sponsor's home. While any person passing by is welcome to attend, the problem, of course, is to locate a performance in the first place.

Your best dance of seeing a full Wayang Kulit in Java is one of the performances sponsored by Radio Republic Indonesia (RRI) on some Saturday

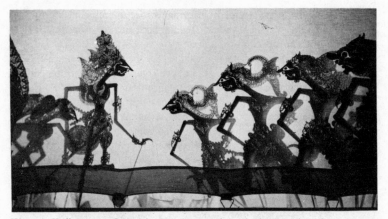

Wayang Kulit puppet figures in Java become lacy shadows against the screen. A formal scene in which the demigod Kresna (left) meets in audience with members of his court.

nights. Bring a sweater or jacket; bring coffee if you can. Sit on the puppet side of the screen (where most Javanese sit these days) to watch musicians and puppeteer and to inspect at close range the magnificent gold-leaf-covered puppets themselves; then move around behind the screen and fall under the spell of Wayang Kulit's hypnotic shadow world. Don't be shy if no one else is watching the shadows; it's the place for connoisseurs. Javanese Wayang Kulit is best seen in Jogjakarta and Surakarta, Central Java.

Balinese *Wayang Kulit*†† lasts four or five hours. It is commonly commissioned as a religious commemoration, one or two nights before a cremation ceremony. Performance is half religious, half entertainment. *Ramayana* stories are popular. Earthy clown figures translate the archaic Kawi language, spoken by aristocratic characters, into colloquial and understandable Balinese. Performance by one puppeteer is basically the same as in Java, but after having seen the Javanese art the Balinese shadow-play seems simple, even crude, in comparison. In my opinion, it is one of Bali's minor dramatic forms.

Doll puppets, *Wayang Golek*†††, are the medium in West Java for dramatizing the same *Mahabharata* and *Ramayana* plays that are performed as shadow- and dance-plays in Central Java. A single puppeteer manipulates rod-doll puppets, speaks dialogue and narration, and sings mood songs; no screen is used; music is by a Sundanese style gamelan, rather faster and livelier in mood than Javanese gamelan; during musical numbers attractive vocalists can be tipped to sing your favorite song, a succession of requests sometimes stopping the show. Wayang Golek performances are commissioned for special occasions, making them hard to find. Regular performances arranged by RRI are excellent and are open to the public.

Indonesian dance-dramas are justly famed for their warm elegance and for the grandeur of their conception; the dance style originated in the courts; music is by a gamelan ensemble. Javanese dance-drama, *Wayang Orang* (also *Wayang Wong*)††††, "human Wayang," has taken the stories, dramatic structure, music, and even some movement techniques from Wayang Kulit. Actor-dancers speak, dance, and also sing; the "puppeteer" remains, but only to chant narrataion between scenes. Week-long programs of Wayang Orang used to be presented at royal courts of princely rulers in Jogjakarta and

Wayang Orang classical dance-drama in Java: the delicate yet powerful hero Ardjuna (played by an actress) fends off a dagger thrust by Tjakil, an ogre who appears in almost every play.

Surakarta until the Second World War; performers and musicians were
court retainers. These lavish spectacles are no more, but there are other ways
you can see classical Wayang Orang style dance and dance-drama. Classical
dance (and gamelan music) are regularly taught in the palaces and at schools,
both government sponsored and private, in the two cities. Rehearsals can
sometimes be attended; watch for occasional public dance concerts or recitals
of excerpts from longer dance dramas.

Then there are 20 to 30 professional troupes that perform commercial
Wayang Orang††† in their own theaters in major cities of Java. The art form

Javanese classical ballet, Sendratari, staged before the
Prambanan Temple complex near Jogjakarta. Sita is receiving
Rama's ring from Hanuman, the white monkey.

is essentially the same as court Wayang Orang—melding dance, song, narrative, and music—but for the popular audience clown scenes have been extended, spectacular staging effects are interpolated, and the dance has been simplified and reduced in importance. A different play nightly; good commercial troupes maintain a high standard of performance. For the visitor with little time, commercial Wayang Orang is probably the most accessible classical Javanese dramatic form (theaters: Sri Wedari in Surakarta, Ngesti Pandawa in Semarang, Pantja Murti in Djakarta).

Finally, newly choreographed ballet spectacles, given the name of *Sendratari*†††, "art-drama-dance," have been created within the past decade for tourist audiences. Dance style and music are traditional; *Ramayana* episodes, which are simple and easy to understand, are used for most ballets; narration and dialogue have been eliminated. We might call Sendratari wordless Wayang Orang. (Theaters: Loro Djonggrang near Jogjakarta; Tjandrawilwatikta Amphitheater, Pandaan, East Java). Balinese, too, have taken up the Sendratari form; half-a-dozen village troupes perform the *Ramayana* in one-hour capsule ballet form for tourist audiences.

The witch Rangda in Balinese Barong is a horrifying figure with projecting fangs, long vibrating fingernails, pendulous breasts, and flames pouring from her mouth.

Traditional dance-dramas in Bali are numerous. The *Barong* trance play†††
is an awe-inspiring ritual enactment of the conflict of good and evil: hideous
Rangda, queen of evil spirits in Bali, battles the beneficient, prancing lion
figure, the Barong. Performance must be arranged if sickness or calamity
strikes a village; that is, when the forces of destruction threaten to overwhelm
the forces of good. After preliminary scenes of dance and dialogue drawn
from episodes of the *Ramayana* and the *Mahabharata*, villagers in deep trance
sweep forward to kill Rangda. But they are helpless against her magical power;
she forces the men to turn their daggers against themselves. The Barong's
power prevents the blades from piercing their flesh; whirling and leaping,
writhing on the ground, the men bend their daggers into curves, forcing them
against their breasts. A Brahman priest sprinkles the cast with holy water;
slowly the performers come out of trance; the ritual enactment is over. A
proper balance between the forces of good and evil is restored, allowing the
village to live again, for a time, in safety. Ritual Barong, difficult to see, is
powerful almost beyond description. Tourists' Barong can be seen almost
every day of the week.

Masked dance-plays are very popular in Bali. *Wayang Topeng*†††, is

In the Balinese Barong dance-drama villagers writhe in trance, pressing their daggers
against their bare chests under the malevolent power of the witch Rangda (here
unseen). Priests enter from the temple to bring the performers out of trance.

based on stories about Javanese Prince Pandji and features a small cast which, with marvelous facility, changes masks throughout the performance as each player takes on a number of roles. (Topeng masked dances and dramatic excerpts are also danced in Sundanese and in Javanese styles on the island of Java, but a visitor rarely has the chance to see a performance.) In *Wayang Wong*††† incidents from the *Ramayana*, and in *Wayang Purwa*††† incidents from the *Mahabharata*, are enacted in parallel dance and musical styles. Performances are quite often seen during Baliness temple festivals. Dance, song, and dialogue combine in all forms of masked Balinese drama.

Ardja†† is a romantic dance-opera. Sentimental stories of separated lovers, abused and reviled, are drawn from legends of East Javanese kingdoms of the twelfth to fifteenth centuries. Professional troupes of actors and actresses are hired for any occasion, but especially for temple festivals. The *Ketjak*††, or "monkey dance," is a strange creation of the 1930s, which is nonetheless impressive and moving. A group of 100–200 men from the village sit on the ground in concentric circles and chant contrapuntally "tjak, tjak, tjak" (the sound of a monkey) as they weave their arms and bodies in unison. If you are the least bit receptive the swelling and ebbing repetitions of sound and movement gradually cast their hypnotic spell. In the center several dancers enact fragments taken from the *Ramayana*, often the abduction of Sita by Ravana. Flickering light from a tier of flaming oil wicks falls on the undulating mass. It is strangely gripping. The monkey chorus is traditional, stemming from trance ritual; the dance episodes were added for audience appeal. Half-a-dozen village groups are proficient in Ketjak.

Legong, Kebyar, and Baris are three fascinating dance forms often seen as items on a dance program. *Legong*††† is a delicate courting dance performed by a pair of preadolescent girls, nymphets who are chaste and sexually appealing at the same instant. *Kebyar*††† is a male solo concert dance, executed entirely in a squatting position; a dance tour de force that emphasizes arm movements and facial expressions; created only two generations ago. *Baris*†† is a male war dance, a group dance that can take a variety of forms, depending upon the circumstances of performance. *Sangyang*†† dancers, either girls or boys, perform in trance on many kinds of religious occasions; they are spirit mediums who contact the gods for blessings and advice.

In Indonesia, traditional theater means puppet-drama and dance-drama. Beginning about one hundred years ago newer, simpler, less sophisticated kinds of drama developed for popular urban audiences. Stories come from recent history (a big hero being Diponegoro, a rebel against Dutch rule), Moslem legends and epics, and from contemporary life. They are dialogue dramas; gamelan music may play in the background; they are not danced; there is nothing "classical" about them; performers ad lib lines from a simple plot synopsis. Professional troupes perform nightly in commercial, and usually

A professional Sandiwara troupe in Djakarta performs the play scene from *Hamlet*, with an actor balancing a beer bottle as part of his act.

squalid, theaters. *Ketoprak*† (or ††) is the popular dramatic form of Central Java. I don't find it a very interesting form myself, but it is easy to find a troupe in Jogjakarta, Surakarta, Semarang, Klaten, Magelang, or other towns where the 25–30 professional troupes play. *Sandiwara*† troupes in West Java stage historical, contemporary, and even Wayang plays; the latter in Sundanese dance-drama style (theaters: Miss Tjitjih's in Djakarta and Sri Murni in Bandung). *Ludruk*† is a strange anomaly: contemporary plays are acted realistically by a cast that includes lurid female impersonators. Surabaya, in East Java, is the center of Ludruk activity; a troupe often performs at Taman Hiburan Rakjat (Peoples' Park) in that city. *Lenong*† is improvised street-theater performed in the Sundanese language in Djakarta. *Dagelan*†, knock-about, ad-libbed, domestic comedy, is popular in the Central Javanese countryside. Both Lenong and Dagelan are rarely seen by visitors. Chinese glove-puppet plays, *Po The Hi*† (or ††) continue to be performed in temple courtyards during Chinese religious festivals; plays are taken from well-known Chinese legends; language of performance is modern Indonesian. *Drama Gong*†† is a new form of spoken drama in Bali; based on traditional stories; with traditional Balinese gamelan music; beautifully costumed; contains no dance at all.

Modern drama attracts the attention of a fair number of the Western educated and elite in Indonesia today. Contemporary plays, modeled on

Sundanese folk-play, Lenong, staged as a dinner show, Hotel Indonesia, Djakarta.
(Photo courtesy Tim Kantoso.)

Western examples, were written and received a good bit of attention following Indonesian Independence in 1949; movies and TV have since absorbed much of the available talent, but interest remains strong in the new drama. The poet W. S. Rendra writes for and directs his Benkel Theater group in experimental plays. There is no professional modern theater in Indonesia.

WHERE TO GO

DJAKARTA. One of the less attractive cities of Asia. Huge (three to five million—no one really knows), sprawling, hot; infuriating traffic, bad public transportation. It has always been a dull theater city, but things are now somewhat improved. The Taman Ismail Marzuki (Djakarta Arts Center) is running full steam; traditional theater can be seen at a few commercial theaters; it is the center for modern drama in the country. At Radio Republic Indonesia you can attend excellent productions of Wayang Orang, first Saturday of the month; Wayang Golek, second Saturday; Sandiwara, third Saturday; and Wayang Kulit, fourth Saturday (if the month has five Saturdays, each form is performed one week later).

Miss Tjitjih's*. A large, dirty, tin shed. Djakarta's only remaining Sandiwara troupe performs here nightly. Seats about 1,500 on slightly raked concrete orchestra level; hard chairs and benches; no air-conditioning; no printed program. Of interest because occasionally they do Wayang stories (*tjerita golek*) here in Sundanese dance-drama style. These are increasingly rare; the usual bill is absurd, ad-libbed contemporary and adventure plays, horror stories, and melodrama. Saturday is always full; otherwise easy to get seats at the door; working-class audience.

Pantja Murti*. Another miserable theater building; small, stuffy, not too clean. Seats 450 in narrow orchestra and tiny balcony; first class has chairs with cushions; no air-conditioning; no printed program. Javanese Wayang Orang is performed nightly by good resident troupe. Chaste, pure, slow, reserved style with more dancing than is usual with commercial troupes. Long, funny clown scenes are well acted; handsome cast; costumes and sets are new and elegant. There used to be four to five Wayang Orang troupes in Djakarta; this is the last one. How long it can continue (houses are seldom full) is a question.

Ramayana Room, Hotel Indonesia***. Each Sunday an "Indonesian Cultural Evening" show with dinner. Bill of folk and classical dance and of dance-drama excerpts from single region of Indonesia; region changes each week. Cast of eight to ten plus gamelan musicians; talented performers; genuine, not hoked up. Held in pleasant, air-conditioned ballroom.

Taman Ismail Marzuki (Djakarta Arts Center)***. The one place for theater in Djakarta you must not miss; very active; site of five theaters, exhibition hall, planetarium, and working rooms for artists. Most nights of the week you can see some modern play, traditional dance-drama, shadow-play, or dance-concert; run is one or two nights only; excellent troupes from around the country are brought in. In my opinion, the most successfully conceived arts center in Asia. Funds which might have gone into a single luxury theater have instead been spent to build five utilitarian and modestly equipped theaters. Every type of performance can be accommodated; running costs are low (so young groups can easily rent); a congenial and encouraging atmosphere for artists.

Teater Besar (Large Theater, also Star Movie House) is air-conditioned; seats 1,200; is used for foreign films primarily; also large-scale dance-drama, foreign visiting troupes, and monthly concert of the Djakarta Symphony Orchestra play here. Warm, intimate **Teater Arena** (Arena Theater) has a central stage area surrounded on four sides by 300 seats; steeply raked for excellent viewing. Folk-drama is often staged here. Back-to-back **Teater Tertutup** (Enclosed Theater) and **Teater Terbuka** (Open-air Theater) can be used simultaneously. Teater Tertutup seats 500; overhead fans; small, 35-foot proscenium stage; mostly for modern drama. Teater Terbuka is an outdoor amphitheater; seats 2,000 on chairs and benches; stadiumlike atmosphere; covered, broad, shallow stage is raised quite high (sit back a few rows for good viewing). Wayang Orang and other dance-dramas play here; for Wayang Kulit, the partition between the two stages is removed and audience can sit in either theater to watch from either side of the screen. The fifth theater is the **Open Air Stage**, a simple platform and backing facing an expanse of lawn; it is seldom used. Printed programs in Indonesian are free; tickets can be purchased either in advance at the Center or at the door.

BALI. The island of Bali, just east of Java, is, as one writer in the 1930s said, "the only happy large community to be seen in the world." This is still true, in spite of the massive international tourist invasion of the past few years. The Balinese exude a sense of exuberant joy in all they do. Life is total for them, evil and good inescapably intertwined. Separating work from play, art from reality, religion from practical life—as we do in the West (and as many other Asians do)—has no place in the Balinese scheme of things. All things are merely the multiple expression of a single life impulse, an impulse that brings man into harmony with his gods and with his natural surroundings. The Balinese celebrate and honor and placate their gods in an endless round of festivals in which, through the tranced bodies of dancers the spirits may return to the Balinese earth to offer advice, ritual dramatic enactments purify the living, and other performances honor the gods and entertain the living. So the natural places in Bali to find theater and dance are temple courtyards, wherever among the island's hundreds of villages there chances to be an Odalan, or temple festival.

Three nights of performance are commonly held in connection with a temple festival, or during the New Year season. At some temples, Bedulu for example, two weeks of performances are not unusual. Cremation is another important, though rare, occasion for major theatrical performances. Festivals go on all day: cockfights in the morning, processions of offerings in the morning and afternoon, religious ceremonies in the afternoon and early evening, and Wayang Wong, Ardja, Wayang Kulit, and other dramatic performances or trance ceremonies at night. Distances are short; you can visit several villages in a day.

Before the jet age ushered in its daily horde of tourists, it was a simple matter to find out about festival performances: each morning the manager of the Bali Hotel in Den Pasar propped up a blackboard and obligingly jotted down the names of choice festivals for that day, including place, and type, and hour of performance. You hired a car, or connived a ride with a friend, or took a bus out to the village, and your day was set. The festivals go on but the blackboard is no longer there. Nowadays, unless you sign up for a tour, people in the tourist business are chary about telling just anybody where festivals are. You must hunt for them on your own as best you can; look up festival dates published in *Indonesia: Important Events* (updated annually); and ask and ask again. Villages with strong traditions of training performers and mounting excellent productions are numerous. The best troupes are invited to perform all over the island. Today there are scores of Legong dancers, more than a dozen Barong groups, perhaps ten Sendratari ballet troupes, half-a-dozen Ketjak groups. Opinions may differ on the quality of performance of many of these, but considered outstanding are: the Ketjak group from Bona; the Baris group at Batur; the Pliatan and Krambitan groups for Legong and other concert-dances; Topeng as performed at Batuan; the Barong at Kuta; and Wayang Kulit performed by puppeteers from Sukawati.

Temple performances are one face of Balinese theater. The other face, the one which every tourist encounters without fail, is the tourist performance. Tourist performances have been around since at least the 1920s. Once a week, or when a passenger ship docked, a selected group of the finest performers were invited to give a gracious and leisurely program of dances in the outdoor pavilion at the Bali Hotel. These occasions were few and the number of performers to choose from large; the performances were but a tiny part of the regular Balinese theatrical scene. Today the hard sell is on. Some 60 travel agencies have signed up 25 village groups to give stripped-down, one-hour tourist shows (after an hour, a tourist gets fidgety, you see). Barong is performed daily at 9:00 A.M. at three or four locations along a single quarter-mile stretch of road between Batubuhlan and Singapadu. Along the "Sanur Strip" (the road leading to Den Pasar from the many hotels at Sanur Beach) 10–12 performance locations have been walled in for evening Ketjak, Legong, and Ramayana Ballet performances; twice, three times a week at each site; some places begin at 6:00 P.M., others at 7:30 P.M., so tourists can catch two shows nightly.

In Den Pasar proper, two or three Ramayana Ballet theaters have been built in recent years; each is open several nights a week. Major hotels also sponsor their own shows, with or without dinner, once or twice weekly; they are usually tastefully presented, if expensive. On the good side, tourist performances are smoothly staged, beautifully costumed, easy to find (look for the signs along the road), and available almost every night of the week. They are the *only* places you can see Legong (and its variation Oleg Tambulilingan), Kebyar, Ketjak, and the Ramayana Ballet; these are secular entertainments and are not a normal part of festival activities. But it is a sad business when one hundred fifty village performers must work to entertain seven or eight spectators and the usual excited throng of Balinese spectators is barred. Balinese are not used to repeating the same play hundreds of times a year. The situation is so artificial that the life has already, after only a few years, gone out of many of these performances; tourist Barong especially is now a travesty of what Barong is in its natural context.

My advice for seeing theater in Bali is: don't worry about what to see. Sample everything you can, festival performances and tourist performances; the best will be thrilling, the worst still better than much you will see elsewhere. You can also go to several theater buildings in Den Pasar where excellent traditional theater is performed for a ticket-buying audience; almost no tourists attend; strongly recommend for convenience and excellence of performing groups.

Konservatori Krawitan or **KOKAR** (Conservatory of Music and Dance)**. A pleasant performance hall at the government performing arts academy in Den Pasar; built in 1960; used by pupils and teachers for special dance-concerts and dance-dramas. The Balinese Sendratari form of Ramayana Ballet was created here (supposedly under the artistic influence of a Javanese dance teacher). Other mixtures of Balinese with Javanese and Sundanese music and dance, which offend some, stem from KOKAR experiments. Unfortunately, only occasional performances are given here.

Lila Buana*. An excitingly designed state theater in Den Pasar. Built in 1971; seats 700 on folding chairs in flat orchestra; not air-conditioned. Evening performances are not advertised; check signboard on front lawn for schedule; inexpensive tickets. Stage has permanent entry doors modeled on Balinese split-arch temple entrance; no scenery; gamelan orchestra sits on side stages. Theater is rented to any type of group, often amateurs; irregular schedule, but two or three performances a week.

Radio Republic Indonesia Studio. A plain theater building in Den Pasar from which RRI broadcasts Wayang Kulit, Wayang Topeng, Ardja, Drama Gong, and other Balinese dramatic forms; every Saturday night and sometimes the night before a holiday. Excellent performances; small admission fee; get your ticket at the door. Seats 600 in wicker basket-chairs set on flat concrete floor; not air-conditioned; comfortable.

Teges Art Center, at Teges Temple, Gianjar District***. Site of occasional spectacular productions of *Wayang Wong Parwa*†††, a reconstructed form of old dance-drama. Actors and actresses speak dialogue, sing, and dance, making this a very interesting type of production. A production requires a half year or more to prepare; irregular scheduling. Performed outdoors before Teges Temple. Inquire in Den Pasar if a performance is scheduled.

BANDUNG. One of Indonesia's most pleasant cities; cool, clean, modern, located high on a mountain plateau four hours by car or train from Djakarta. Capital of West Java Province and center of Sundanese culture. A dozen Sundanese-language Sandiwara troupes play in Bandung and neighboring towns. Wayang Golek is broadcast at the Bandung RRI studio the first

Saturday evening of each month; open to the public for a small admission fee. One Javanese-language Wayang Orang troupe has been here for 20 years. Theaters are dirty and uncomfortable. No printed information about theater activity; inquire.

Sri Murni*. A miserable, smelly little place, but the chief Sandiwara troupe in Bandung plays here. Seats 400 on orchestra level in hard chairs and benches; no air-conditioning. Awful historical or contemporary plays Monday through Saturday; interesting Wayang dance-drama Sunday. Buy ticket at door.

Suryodadari*. An unpleasant shed-theater; perhaps a bit better than Sri Murni, but something to be put up with nonetheless. Seats 550 on cane-bottomed chairs and benches in flat orchestra. Wayang Orang performed in Javanese language nightly; troupe is not particularly exciting though the clowns are good; simple, straightforward style of performance; house is seldom full.

JOGJAKARTA. A marvelously atmospheric, relaxing city, where people quietly revere and practice the old traditions of Javanese arts; not an exciting city, but a deeply satisfying one for those who will take the time to absorb and savor Jogjakarta's uniquely placid ambience. Catch any performance of classical dance or dance-drama that may be given by the two big dance schools—Akademi Seni Tari Indonesia or Krido Bekso Wiromo. Do try to be in Jogjakarta the second Saturday of the month: RRI sponsors a superb all-night Wayang Kulit performance open to the public (theater: Sosono Hinggil). Part of each year a large temporary theater will be set up in the Alun-alun Lor (North Palace Square) and visiting Wayang Orang and Ketoprak troupes stay on for several months performing nightly; just walk down to the square and see if a theater is there.

In case you can't see classical Javanese theater any other way, short dance- and shadow-play excerpts are staged each week at several locations for tourists; see *Welcome to Jogjakarta* listings. Week-long Sekaten festival (April or May) draws hundreds of thousands of Javanese to Jogjakarta in honor of the birthday of the Prophet Mohammad. North Palace Square is jammed with booths, sideshows, food stalls, games, and one or two theaters. Two palace gamelan ensembles play alternately day and night through the week in front of the Mesdjid Agung (Great Mosque) fronting the square. On the seventh day, known as Grebeg, a long procession enacting the lost panoply of the royal court winds out of the palace gate into the square; some years the palace will sponsor a royal Wayang Kulit performance in the Alun-alun Kidul (South Palace Square) open to the public.

Gedung Pertemuan Batik (Batik Cooperative Hall, also called PPBI

Hall)**. A privately owned rental hall; seats 700 in stepped orchestra; fairly comfortable; no air-conditioning; lacks adequate lighting. Is used primarily for meetings, recitals, and concerts of dance, both classical Javanese and Western. Conveniently close to North Palace Square.

Loro Djonggrang Outdoor Theater ***. Located at Klaten on the road from Jogjakarta to Surakarta. Outdoor theater which is the site of the annual summer Ramayana Ballet Festival each month June through October for four nights during the full moon. Lit by floodlights, Loro Djonggrang Temple (better known as Prambanan) makes a stunningly beautiful backdrop above the low stage that seems as broad as a football field, but is really only half that large; formal temple archways frame stage entrances. A huge cast of dancers enact the *Ramayana* in four consecutive episodes; hundreds of girls and boys in continuous motion depict armies of giants, snakes, swimming fishes, and licking flames. Everyone likes the little boy monkeys who scratch, cavort, turn somersaults, and generally try to steal as much of the show as they can get away with. Choreography is massive and spectacular; costuming is splendid. The best dancers from Jogjakarta and Surakarta no longer perform; some dancing has become sloppy; nonetheless, all except the most particular should enjoy this major dance attraction in Indonesia. Steeply raked bleachers running the length of the stage seat 1,000; recommend expensive center seats; tickets available at tourist agencies; buy in advance for a good seat. The Prambanan Temple complex should not be missed; go during the daytime to examine *Ramayana* episodes carved in relief around the ambulatory of Loro Djonggrang Temple.

Sosono Hinggil**. Government-owned hall in which Radio Republic Indonesia holds its monthly Wayang Kulit broadcast performances. A simple hall; seats 600 on a level orchestra; not air-conditioned. The screen is on the stage and the puppeteer has his back to the audience. You can sit in a regular orchestra seat, or go behind the screen by yourself, sit, and watch the shadows. As long as you do not make noise or otherwise disturb the performers it's all right to be there.

Taman Hiburan Rakjat (People's Amusement Park)**. A permanent commercial theater usually occupied by touring Ketoprak or Wayang Orang. The standard, dirty, urban concrete theater with corrugated-iron roof; no air-conditioning; one side is open to let the breeze through. This is a noisy theater; it is beside the city bus terminal.

SURAKARTA (also called *SOLO*).   With Jogjakarta, one of two ancient court cities of Central Java. Historically older than its rival to the west, the arts of Surakarta are light and gay, while those of Jogjakarta are more somber and conservative. Commercial Wayang Orang troupes took their inspiration from lively Surakarta style court dance and music; the audience-appealing trick of having refined male roles played by attractive actresses is a Surakarta idea. Visitors may watch classical *Bedaya* court dances†††† being rehearsed in the Surakarta palace each fifth Tuesday morning (Selasa Kliwon by the Javanese calendar); inquire for permission to attend. See Wayang Kulit broadcast performance at RRI studio, third Saturday evening of the month; open to the public for a nominal fee. The Museum Radya Pustaka, next to Sri Wedari Park, has a large and extremely interesting collection of Javanese puppets: traditional Wayang Purwa shadow-puppets for *Mahabharata* and *Ramayana* plays; Wayang Gedog puppets for *Pandji* plays; Wayang Klitik shadow-puppets made of wood; and, high on the walls, rare Wayang Beber paper scrolls that were unrolled to perform *Pandji* plays. Surakarta is small and easy to get around in by betjak; no printed theater information.

Sri Wedari **. A must. The permanent Sri Wedari troupe that performs here nightly is considered Indonesia's finest commercial Wayang Orang group. Physically one of the better commercial theater buildings, though it is still just a shed theater; clean; open on the sides for coolness; large and airy; seats 1,200 on gently sloping orchestra; large, comfortable wicker chairs in first class; no printed program. Almost always SRO; recommend you walk over to the theater and get your ticket around 6:00–7:00 P.M. (it is close to hotels). Ask for "Wayang Orang" at ticket window at left side of entrance to Sri Wedari Amusement Park; your theater ticket lets you into the park as well.

Books to Read

GENERAL: James R. Brandon, *Theatre in Southeast Asia* (Cambridge, Mass.: Harvard University Press, 1967); Claire Holt, *Art in Indonesia* (Ithaca, N.Y.: Cornell University Press, 1967); James L. Peacock, *Rites of Modernization: Symbolic and Formal Aspects of Indonesian Proletarian Drama* (Chicago: University of Chicago Press, 1968); H. Ulbricht, *Wayang Purwa: Shadows of the Past* (London: Oxford University Press, 1970); Beryl de Zoete and Walter Spies, *Dance and Drama in Bali* (London: Faber and Faber, 1952).

PLAYS: James R. Brandon, ed., *On Thrones of Gold: Three Javanese Shadow Plays* (Cambridge, Mass.: Harvard University Press, 1970).

Japan

J apan is the theatergoer's paradise. Traditional drama, puppet-theater, dance-plays, modern drama, and musicals, to say nothing of village folk performances, go on side by side. There are so many kinds of plays and so many performances that it is impossible to see everything. Theater facilities are splendid and getting to the theater is as easy as anywhere in Asia. The best types of drama dazzle with their sophisticated artistry. A day, a week, a year—10 years—could be spent enjoyably seeing plays in this supremely interesting country.

An island nation, Japan is relatively small and isolated from other countries. Its people developed an extremely homogeneous culture so that the theater is basically the same from one region to another. Interesting folk performances can be seen in the countryside, but there are no regional theater forms so significant that a visit to the hinterlands is a necessity (as in India, Indonesia, or Thailand). You can see virtually everything in Tokyo. Almost maddeningly animated, it is the center of Japanese theater—as New York is the center of American theater. Regular productions are staged in Osaka, Kyoto, and Nagoya—some locally produced, but the majority on tour out of Tokyo (always with the original cast, by the way). Troupes occasionally tour to lesser cities: Hiroshima, Fukuoka, Takamatsu, Sendai, Niigata, Sapporo.

Theater is highly commercial. Two theatrical combines, Shochiku and Toho, own a score of theaters and manage a dozen of the most important theater troupes. Pickup casts are becoming increasingly common, but the troupe system remains an inescapable part of Japanese theater. All performances are in Japanese. Do not be fooled; though Japan is the most modernized country in Asia, in spite of appearances it is not Westernized. Fewer people will speak English than you might expect (fortunately most theater switchboard operators do). A great attraction about Japanese culture and all of its arts is that the old is not abandoned in favor of the new. Almost anything you might wish to see in the theater is there: from classic Noh to *Fiddler on the Roof.*

THEATERGOING

Going to a play is an excursion. Theaters are located in the heart of an entertainment area, surrounded by restaurants, bars, night clubs, coffee shops, movie houses. Playbills last four or five hours. It is expected that you will eat and drink during this time; 30-minute intermissions between acts are common; relax and take in the scene. A troupe does two shows a day at most traditional theaters: matinee from 11:00 or 11:30 A.M. and evening performance from 4:00 or 4:30 P.M. Matinee and evening bills are different and each consists of three, four, or five plays (or, in the case of Kabuki and Bunraku, selected acts from longer plays). At a single theater, then, it is possible to watch 10 hours of plays a day, if your constitution is strong enough. For most modern drama, there is a single performance, beginning at 6:00 or 6:30 P.M. By 10:00 P.M. theaters are dark and the streets quickly become deserted, except for night owls looking for late bars.

THEATER BUILDINGS. Most theaters were destroyed by bombing in the Second World War. Some were rebuilt in traditional style: square-shaped auditoriums with the stage opening extending the width of the building, and shallow U-shaped balconies circling the auditorium, so that the center of the building is completely open. In the older theaters you can kneel, as audiences did centuries ago, in special sections (*sajiki*) covered with straw matting. Within the past fifteen years a score of new, magnificently equipped, luxurious theater structures have been built; some of the finest theater buildings in the world are now found in Japan. These follow the Western pattern: fan-shaped auditorium, smaller stage opening, and balcony that projects quite far forward. Important theaters will have five or six restaurants (where you can eat a full meal during a long intermission), snack bars, and souvenir counters selling fans, records, and books. Opera glasses are for rent, and illustrated programs in Japanese (and sometimes English) are inexpensive. Ticket prices are the highest in Asia, but worth it, with first class over US$10 for some performances. While it is generally possible to buy a ticket at the box office at curtain time, good performances can be SRO, or the whole house may be sold out to a theater party, in which case there is no way to get a ticket. Most theaters accept direct phone reservations; you can buy in advance at an agent in your hotel, or at a Play Guide in a department store (no commission is charged). Taking pictures, with or without flash, is strictly forbidden in major theaters.

SEASON.   Theaters run year-round in Japan although the importance of performances tapers off in July and August when star performers are on holiday. November–February is the height of the season. There is no long-run system; major commercial theaters, including those that stage Kabuki and other legitimate drama, change their bills monthly: twenty-five consecutive days of performance is followed, at the end of the month, by four or five dark days during which the next month's bill is rehearsed. Smaller theaters with smaller audiences schedule runs for a few days or a week. Without exception, a bill of Noh plays will be given a single performance only.

FESTIVALS.   The Japanese love nature, and the theme and mood of a play will match the season (a love play in spring, a melancholy play in the fall), but the scheduling of most major performances is independent of seasonal festivals. Nor are national festivals important. The Osaka International Festival, held annually in March and April, has become one of the major music, ballet, and theater events on the international scene and is attended by tourists from all over the world. See your travel agent.

TRANSPORTATION.   Cruising taxis are everywhere in the day and early evening; metered; no tipping. They tend to disappear after 10:00 P.M. Most rides to a theater will run a dollar or two. Drivers are honest but do not speak English; either learn to pronounce the Japanese name of the theater correctly or, better, have your hotel clerk write it in Japanese. Public transportation goes everywhere. Subways and surface interurban railways lace the cities; they are cheap and stations have their names in Roman letters. Highly recommended except during rush hours, when they are horrendously crowded. Streetcars in Kyoto work well, too. Forget buses: signs are in Japanese characters and you will never know where they are going. Street signs, in Roman letters, mark downtown streets in Osaka, Kyoto, and Nagoya; in Tokyo some streets are marked and some are not. Walking can be a joy. Crowds are dense but the jostle and pulse of the city streets has its own charm. Streets are completely safe day or night. Train service between cities in Japan is excellent and not expensive. Special "Bullet" express trains go from Tokyo to Kyoto or Osaka in three hours. Japan Travel Bureau (JTB) makes up tours to some festivals and regional folk performances.

INFORMATION.   One of the pleasures of going to the theater in Japan is that it is relatively easy to find out what is going on and where. Major performances are listed daily in four English newspapers (the *Japan Times*, the *Daily Yomiuri*, the *Asahi Evening News*, and *Mainichi Daily News*). Carried as a service and expanded or reduced to accomodate space, no single day's list of theaters is complete; the *Mainichi* carries relatively detailed information, making it your first choice to buy at a newsstand. The Saturday *Japan Times* columns "Theater Off Ginza" (modern drama and avant-garde) and "What is On Next Week" (Noh and Kyogen) are useful. Of the half-dozen tourist magazines and tabloids usually available free in hotels, several have useful information: *Japan Visitor's Guide* (excellent maps and listings of most traditional plays); *Tour Companion* (unusual festival performances are featured in each issue) and *Tokyo Total: Entertainment Guide* (commercial theater listings and articles on theater). Theater ads rarely appear in English-language publications. The monthly schedule of the Kanze Noh school in Tokyo and in Kyoto is sometimes left at hotels; look carefully and you will see play titles, dates, and hours in English. Two nationally circulated Japanese-language magazines carry schedules of almost everything (except Noh) playing in Tokyo, Kyoto, Osaka, and Nagoya: *Engekikai*, found on some newsstands (see its last few pages) and *Shukan Shincho*, sold everywhere (see "Stage" and "Show Business" pages in front). Get your hotel clerk to translate and to telephone. For information on festivals, phone or go to the Japan National Tourist Organization: in Tokyo on Harumidori, between Hibiya Subway station and the railroad overpass (1, Yurakucho, Chiyoda-ku) or, in Kyoto in the Kyoto Tower Building in front of Kyoto Station (Higashi Shiokojicho, Shimogyo-ku). They are invariably helpful and responsive to requests. You can buy many books on Japanese theater at bookstores.

WHAT TO SEE

Stately *Bugaku*†††† court dances were brought to Japan from Korea and China thirteen hundred years ago. At shrines and at the Imperial Palace on auspicious occasions they are still performed in brilliantly costumed splendor to Chinese-derived ethereal music of flutes, drums, lute, zither, and panpipe. In recent years public performances have been given in Tokyo twice a year (Kokuritsu Gekijo, small theater). Even more ancient are native ritual dances, *Kagura* (literally "god dance")†† performed to honor local Shinto deities. The dancer is either a young boy or, more often, a shrine maiden dressed in white, the color of purity. The gods are honored through dance, and contact with them is established by the living (a shamanistic belief). Different types of Kagura can be seen performed at Shinto shrine festivals in different parts of Japan.

Masked *Noh*†††† dance-drama carries the spectator into the austere world of medieval Japan, in which the spirits of unhappy warriors and court ladies suffer until redeemed by the love of Amida Buddha. Noh plays are performed in elegant simplicity (the influence of Zen Buddhism) on a bare stage with a minimum of properties. Accompanied by just three drums and a flute, the voices of the actors and seated chorus rise and fall in somber chant and rhythmic song. So slow are the perfectly controled movements of the actors' arms and white-socked feet, restrained by encompassing robes of brocade, that time seems suspended. Incredibly beautiful and moving are the masks, their emotions held in subtle repose, as if a crude feeling would shatter the other-worldly image created in our mind's eye.

From a rustic village entertainment, Noh was transformed into a serious Buddhist art by the performer Kannami Kiyotsugu in the fourteenth century, and by his son Zeami Motokiyo into a refined and splendid court art in the fifteenth century. From that time until the Meiji restoration (1868), Noh was an exclusive art of the ruling samurai (warrior) class. A day's program in Zeami's time consisted of at least five plays—a god play, a warrior play, a woman play, a possession play, and a demon play—interspersed with gently comic *Kyogen*†††† plays for a change of pace. Today the usual bill is two or three Noh (each lasting about an hour) and one or two Kyogen (lasting about 30–40 minutes). Based on master-servant, husband-wife, country bumpkin–city slicker confrontations, Kyogen are spoken dialogue farce-comedies that bubble with good humor. Where Noh is sublime, Kyogen is infinitely human.

Noh is performed in major cities in special indoor theaters that are owned and operated by five Noh organizations or schools (Kanze, Hosho, Komparu,

Izutsu, a Noh play at the Kanze Nogakudo, Tokyo. (Photo courtesy Andrew Tsubaki.)

A modern Kyogen comedy, but performed on a traditional Noh stage and using traditional movements.

Kongo, and Kita). A Noh bill is performed just once. At each theater there will be one "regular" school-sponsored performance (*teiki Noh*) each month, starring leading Noh performers of that school, plus recital-performances 15–20 times a month by lesser actors, including student amateurs. Regular performances may be advertised in English publications; usually SRO; order a ticket in advance. Tickets can cost US$10 or more; the more expensive the ticket, the higher-ranking the actor. Although theaters are small (200–400), side seats have poor viewing; buy center section if you can afford it. (Theaters: Tokyo: Kanze Nogakudo, Nakano Umewaka Gakuin Kaikan, Suidobashi Nohgakudo, Yarai Nogakudo, Kita Nohgakudo; Kyoto: Kyoto Kanze Kaikan, Kongo Nogakudo, Oe Nogakudo.) In addition, Noh plays are performed on various festival occasions throughout Japan, on outdoor stages, often quite ancient, that are built in the precincts of Shinto shrines and Buddhist temples. These festival performances can be during the day, or at night lighted by blazing bonfires (*takigi* Noh, "torchlight Noh").

Kabuki†††† has been Japan's popular theater for three centuries. It is as flamboyant as Noh is restrained, as colorful as Noh is subdued, as raucously humorous as Noh is somber. Kabuki began as scandalous, sensuous dance. Constantly altering its form in response to changes in Japanese society, Kabuki has assimilated parts of Noh dance-plays and Bunraku puppet techniques, and has developed a unique gangster genre of play (that later became the basis of Japanese sword-fighting movies). In a dozen clangorous commercial theaters during the Edo period (1600–1868), Kabuki actors gave marathon performances in plays that ran from dawn to dusk. Plays were divided into history, dance, and domestic sections. Today, the usual Kabuki program lasts five hours, and is divided into the same history-dance-domestic sequence.

Kabuki is spectacular; grandiose sets change on a revolving stage or rise on an elevator before your eyes; actors move through the audience on a rampway (*hanamichi*, "flower way") leading to the stage from the rear of the auditorium; costumes, wigs, and makeup are strikingly colorful; music of drums, gongs, bells, and three-stringed *shamisen* accompany intricately stylized battle scenes; songs set the mood of a scene; wooden clappers beat furious tattoos of sound as an actor rushes on or off stage. Highlights of the actor's art are the dynamic windup of the body and the *mie* (pose) during a climactic moment, and the soaring cadences of rhythmically spoken speeches. Today, Kabuki is touted as a "classic" art, but don't be awed by that. Kabuki is meant to be enjoyed; sit back and let its sensuality of sight and sound flood over you.

You have a choice of two to three Kabuki productions each month of the year; they are widely advertised and will be easy to locate. Most performances are in Tokyo; Kyoto, Osaka, and Nagoya also host productions two or three months each. The biggest production of the year is *kaomise*, "face showing," which traditionally begins the new Kabuki season. Kaomise performances are in May (Osaka: Shin Kabukiza); October (Nagoya: Misonoza); November (Tokyo: Kabukiza); and December (Kyoto: Minamiza). Actors to watch for are Onoe Shoroku, Onoe Baiko, Nakamura Utaemon, Nakamura Ganjiro, Nakamura Kanzaburo, Matsumoto Koshiro. Popular younger actors are Ichikawa Ebizo, Bando Tamasaburo, Onoe Tatsunosuke, Onoe Kikugoro. (Theaters: Tokyo: Kabukiza, Kokuritsu Gekijo [large theater], and sometimes Shimbashi Embujo, Toyoko Gekijo, Teikoku Gekijo, and Kokuritsu Gekijo [small theater]; Kyoto: Minamiza; Osaka: Shin Kabukiza; Nagoya: Misonoza and Chunichi Gekijo.)

Bunraku†††† is a complex puppet-theater that grew up as a popular art at about the same time and under the same circumstances as Kabuki. In fact, many Bunraku plays are done by Kabuki actors. Three manipulators operate one puppet, moving arms and fingers, legs, body, head, eyes, mouth, and even eyebrows so realistically you soon forget the actors are made of wood and cloth. While the doll-puppets are moved, one chanter (occasionally augmented by others) sings narration and speaks dialogue; he is accompanied by the deeply emotional music of the plucked shamisen. All of this is placed on a regular stage, about three-quarters normal size. At times 30–40 puppeteers, chanters, and musicians are in full view. Listen as the chanter slaps his reading

Three Misfits, a comic Kabuki dance-play, adapted from a medieval Kyogen comedy. Singers and shamisen players perform on stage. (Photo courtesy Shochiku Theater Co.)

desk, his lips quivering in anguish, his voice rising in a hoarse wail; puppet figures sob with grief, eyebrows vibrating, eyes blinking, and jointed fingers clenched in pain. Actions and voices come at you from several directions; in the end they fuse; the experience is intensely emotional while the technique is one of exceptional virtuosity.

Bunraku is an Osaka art and its best plays reflect the pragmatic, yet highly romantic, view of the Osaka merchant class that patronized puppet-drama. Chikamatsu Monzaemon (1653–1724) wrote domestic tragedies about young merchants and their courtesan lovers forced to commit double suicide. History plays celebrate the intense feudal loyalty of mothers and fathers who voluntarily, but in deep anguish, sacrifice a young son or daughter to protect their lord. Plays fairly drip with the blood of tragic death.

At one time a dozen troupes performed puppet drama; this has dwindled to a single troupe, partially subsidized by the Ministry of Education. It plays four times a year in its home theater, the Asahiza, in Osaka (January, April, July–August and October) and at the Kokuritsu Gekijo (small theater) in Tokyo four times a year (February, May–June, September, and November) for runs of two weeks or more. Daily matinee and evening performances of different bills.

Shimpa†† is "new school" drama in distinction to traditional Kabuki. It is sentimental melodrama based on late nineteenth- and early twentieth-century Western popular drama that was first introduced to Japan soon after the Meiji Restoration. It was startlingly new, and exotic, then. Shimpa actresses were the first women to appear on the stage in 250 years (only men perform Noh, Kabuki, Bunraku). Shimpa plays took up all the recent exciting events of the day and looked at them through the eyes of the middle class: There is no violence in Shimpa drama. Today, productions retain the spirit of a past era. They are boring to some, quaintly charming to others. Shimpa is performed by a single troupe led by a superbly talented actress, Mizutani Yaeko. Two bills daily; several plays on each bill; different bills at a different theater each month. (Theaters: Tokyo: Shimbashi Embujo, Meijiza, or Nissei Gekijo; Osaka: Shin Kabukiza; Kyoto: Minamiza; Nagoya: Misonoza.)

Shinkokugeki††, "new national drama," is a modern offshoot of Kabuki. Exciting and extended scenes of sword-fighting, often against a rear-projected movie of the battle, are a specialty of the one troupe doing Shinkokugeki. A minor form of drama. Two shows daily; several plays on each program; monthly change of bill. (Theaters: Tokyo: Koma Gekijo, Meijiza, or Shimbashi Embujo.)

Tabishibai†, "traveling show," are fourth-rate little troupes that can still be found playing in miserable shacks on the outskirts of major cities. They try to copy Kabuki acting style and steal its plays. Most troupes are utterly without talent. It's chancy finding them; their theaters aren't very permanent. Not for the fastidious. (Theater: Tokyo: Shinohara Engeijo.)

Traditional storytellers are marvelously entertaining. *Rakugo*††† is the art of the comic storyteller, who kneels on a cushion, formally dressed in kimono and cloak, and recounts a 20–30 minute tale. He mugs, mimes with fan and towel, and tells elaborate puns (which you will wish you could understand). *Kodan*†† performers recite in emotional tones the old epic tales of samurai battles. *Manzai*† two-man (or -woman) vaudeville teams sing and tell jokes. Some bills at traditional Yose, or "variety halls," contain only Rakugo or Kodan. Other programs include, Rakugo, Kodan, Manzai, and a juggler, paper cutter, Chinese magician, song-and-dance artists, and other variety acts as well. Rarely will you see another foreigner at a variety hall. Some of these small special theaters are new and modern; some reek with traditional atmosphere. Performers do a different routine each day of a 10-day run; the line-up for a bill changes every ten days. You will see 12–15 acts on each bill. (Theaters: Tokyo: Suehirotei, Toho Meijinkai, Asakusa Engei Horu, Suzumoto Engeijo, Honmokutei, Mokubakan, Shochiku Engeijo; Osaka: Kadoza.)

Modern drama based on Western models is *Shingeki*†††, literally "new drama." It developed under the influence of Tolstoy, Chekhov, Stanislavsky, and Ibsen, and today remains a serious, ideological, socially conscious, literary art form. It has never been merely entertainment. Major Western plays are done in translation and scores of original Shingeki plays are written each year. Suppressed during the Second World War by the Japanese government, Shingeki flourished in the postwar years. Its audience is elite, not large enough to support Shingeki professionally. Actors subsist by working in the mammoth movie and television industries. Small troupes constantly form and disband. Established, respected troupes are: Bungakuza (Literary Theater), led by actress Sugimura Haruko, nonideological and classic-oriented; Haiyuza (The Actor's Theater), which has produced a number of important actors; Kumo (Cloud), led by Shakespearean director Senda Koreya and featuring the exciting actress Kishida Kyoko; Mingeiza (Peoples' Art Theater), a socially committed, progressive troupe; and Shiki (Four Seasons), specializing in brilliantly acted translations of French drama. Somewhat more popularly-oriented, NLT (National Literary Theater) has produced most of the late Mishima Yukio's modern plays. (A modern drama troupe like Toho's Gendai Gekidan [Modern Drama Troupe] isn't considered real Shingeki because its plays are light drama—like Broadway or West End pot-boilers, "mere entertainment.") Shingeki plays run a few nights or as long as a month; the average is about two weeks; one performance nightly. Not widely publicized in English publications; tickets are sold at Play Guides. (Theaters: Tokyo: Haiyuza, Nissei Gekijo, Toyoko Gekijo, Kinokuniya Horu; Osaka: Nakaza; Kyoto: Kyoto Kaikan, Kyoto Furitsu Kaikan; Nagoya: Chunichi Gekijo, Meitetsu Horu; and small theaters as well.)

Girls' Opera†† holds a strange position in Japanese theater. More than a mere novelty, it has developed in the past 40 years into a special form with definite characteristics. In style it is saccharine and sexless; its audience is 95 percent female. Singing and dancing are well executed; adaptations of traditional dance and theater (Noh, Kabuki), folk dances, and modern musical revue materials all are staged; scenic effects are spectacular; costumes are lavishly beautiful. Girls' Opera is performed by half-a-dozen permanent troupes of 100–150 performers. (Theaters: Tokyo: Takarazukaza, Shinjuku Koma Gekijo, and Kokusai Gekijo; Osaka: Takarazukaza; Nagoya: Chunichi Gekijo.)

Musical Revues†† have been popular in Japan since the 1920s. Three or four are playing at all times; intricately staged; expensively costumed; very ordinary popular music and uninspired choreography. Performers are undoubtedly talented, but from a Western point of view they somehow lack that vital spark that marks a star singer-dancer in musical theater. There is

An all-girl, modern, musical review at the Kokusai Gekijo in Tokyo uses lavish costumes and setting on an enormous stage. (Photo courtesy Kokusai Gekijo.)

a blandness in Japanese musicals that is not displeasing, but it certainly is not very exciting either. (Theaters: Tokyo: Nihon Gekijo and Shinjuku Koma Gekijo some months; Osaka: Umeda Koma Gekijo.)

Musical Comedies†††, usually American musicals translated into Japanese, are a recent craze. *Fiddler on the Roof*, *Oklahoma*, *Fantastiks*, *My Fair Lady*, *Applause*, and others have been stylishly produced with excellent, talented, young casts. Well worth seeing; will be advertised; no special theaters.

Avant-Garde†† (or †††) theater is alive and well; some claim the first Happening happened in Tokyo. Young people play in tents on open lots, under train tracks, in tiny basement rooms, with a zest and dedication unmatched by their elders in more traditional theater forms. Marvelous makeup; an actor slides down a rope or swings on a trapeze; riotously satiric songs assault and entertain you; sometimes sexually and physically shocking; never dull. The level of creativity fluctuates, but is generally high. Performances are sporadically arranged and are often in strange and hard-to-find places. Chief groups are Kara Juro's Jokyo Gekijo (sometimes called the Red Tent Theater), Terayama Shuji's Tenjosajiki (Peanut Gallery Theater), the studio group of Abe Kobo, and Waseda Shogekijo (Waseda Little Theater) that specializes in far-out adaptations of traditional plays. (Theaters: Tokyo: Tenjo Sajikikan, Jean-Jean, and Shinjuku Bunka.)

Foreign ballet, opera, music, and drama troupes often visit Japan and perform in Tokyo and Osaka. Except for the Osaka International Festival in March–April, no special time or place; visits are advertised widely.

WHERE TO GO

Tokyo has 30 large, important theaters and twice that many small theaters and performance halls. There are a dozen theaters in Osaka; half that number in Kyoto and in Nagoya. Special festival performances can be seen in the streets or at temples and shrines in these four cities and elsewhere.

TOKYO. Fast-moving, up-to-date, intense, an incredibly vital city. The smog now rivals Los Angeles' and the traffic can be frightening. The theater, however, is great. Theaters cluster in five big entertainment districts of the city, each with its own particular atmosphere: downtown Ginza-Yurakucho; upper-middle-class Shibuya; trendy, young, experimental Shinjuku; and Ueno and Asakusa, mercantile and wholesale areas that retain a strong spirit of older Japan. Glittering and expensive Ginza and the working man's gaudy Asakusa are worlds apart (though only 30 minutes by train). Dramatic masks, dance fans, and Kabuki acting properties, such as swords, are sold in many stores. The **Tsubouchi Memorial Museum**, Waseda University, housed in a Shakespearean theater, is the country's finest theatrical library and collection; models of Japanese theaters and puppets from all parts of Asia are especially interesting.

Asakusa Engei Horu (Asakusa Variety Hall)**. A 355-seat converted movie-house featuring young variety performers; clean; comfortable; air-conditioned. This is a surprisingly good Yose, with a warm atmosphere and lively entertainers.

Geijitsuza (Art Theater)***. In Yurakucho district. A small theater; seats 710 on one floor; stage is 45 feet wide; air-conditioned; comfortable; printed Japanese program; snacks. Home of the Toho Modern Drama Troupe (Toho Gendai Gekidan), perhaps better called the "Toho Modern Soap Opera Troupe." Genre plays, plays of human interest, plays "with a heart," for a middle-class "Wednesday matinee" audience. A play runs two or three months, depending on its popularity. Because the house is long and narrow you don't want to be too far back. Unless the play is exceptional, tickets are overpriced in my opinion.

Haiyuza (Actors' Theater)**. The first theater building to belong to a Shingeki troupe and the first to be built after the war. Haiyuza has hosted many famous postwar modern-drama productions, but it is now becoming a bit seedy and sad. You are close to the stage from any of the 450 seats in the orchestra and small balcony. Strictly a functional theater; narrow seats; not very comfortable; no restaurant; no opera glasses; no fancy decor;

Japanese-language program. The Haiyuza Troupe stages its own, usually very fine, productions three or four times a year for three-week runs. They have staged more than one hundred productions so far. Young, experimental groups rent the rest of the time. Minor plays run three or four days.

Honmokutei (Honmoku Variety Hall)**. Newly rebuilt (1972) variety hall in Ueno; very comfortable; air-conditioned; small; normally rents to amateur groups. Each bill devoted to one form: Kodan, Rakugo, Manzai, singing to shamisen, women's puppet narration, and others.

Jean-Jean**. A tiny avant-garde theater in the basement of Tokyo Yamate Church in Shibuya. Pedestal bucket chairs in L-shaped arrangement facing a minuscule thrust stage. Minimal lighting and staging effects. Air-conditioned; comfortable; no reserved seats. A rental house. Experimental plays, often with exceptional casts, poetry readings, song recitals, rock concerts; runs of one to three nights.

Kabukiza (Kabuki Theater)****. The Grand Dame of Tokyo theater houses; in the East Ginza district. Built in 1887 and reconstructed many times since, most recently in 1951 after being bombed out during the war. Baroque and impressive; many new theaters now surpass its once unequalled elegance; air-conditioned; seats 2,216 in wide orchestra (sajiki along sides)

Kabukiza, Tokyo.

and two balconies. Buy either first- or third-class ticket; second class is far away but still expensive; use opera glasses in balconies; all seats reserved; often SRO. Some performances sold en bloc to firms; wise to phone. Many foreign spectators here; English information desk in lobby. Huge 93-foot stage opening; hanamichi; revolving stage; elevators. Monthly bill, usually from the first or second for 26 consecutive days. Matinee and evening bills are different and contain three to five items each. On opening day each month your ticket is good all day. Opening day in January is like a festival: women dress in their best New Year's kimono, and sport old-style hairdos; even men may wear kimono. Kabuki plays January, February, April, May, July, and November and occasionally March, September, and October as well. Casts are superior; staging is magnificent. What a shame this great theater is wasted on trivia other months. Six restaurants; detailed English programs and books on Kabuki sold at the door; Kabuki records and souvenirs sold inside; opera glasses for rent. Tickets are expensive. For a cheap ticket, to see a single play from the last two rows of the upper balcony, go around to the entryway at the left of the main entrance. (Obviously, you have to know which play you want to see on the bill and you have to know what time it begins; this makes sense only if you are desperate for money and you have good vision.) Across the street a record shop sells a large selection of Kabuki, Noh, Kyogen, and Bunraku records.

Kanze Nogakudo (Kanze Noh Theater)****. A luxurious and modern temple dedicated to the art of Noh. In middle-class Shibuya district. Built 1971; modernist design outside; auditorium and stage fairly shine with brightness. Seats 425 in ten rows center and left; air-conditioned; very comfortable seating. Regular Kanze school performances in Tokyo are held here first Sunday of each month; usual bill is four Noh, two or three Kyogen, and several Noh dance excerpts (*shimai*). Performances by lesser artists several times weekly. Few performances in August. The theater publishes a monthly schedule in Japanese that contains small-print English translations of play titles, dates, and hours of performances.

Kinokuniya Horu (Kinokuniya Hall)***. A plain theater in Shinjuku area where some interesting modern drama can be seen. Mishima Yukio's plays have been staged here as well as exciting experiments combining Noh, Kyogen, and Shingeki in a single production. A long (22 rows), narrow house seating 440; air-conditioned; reasonably comfortable seats; no restaurant; Japanese-language program. This is a rental house and the quality of performance varies widely depending on the troupe; runs last a week or two; one performance daily. Young, intellectual audience.

Kokuritsu Gekijo (National Theater of Japan)****. An impressive modern structure, covering a city block. Built by the government in 1966, it is half a mile from the Ginza overlooking the Imperial Palace moat. Contains a large theater seating 1,850 used primarily for Kabuki and a small theater that seats about 400 used for Bunraku, Bugaku court dances, classical dance recitals, and other programs. Chastely appointed, even severe, it is a magnificent theatrical mechanism; equipped with a TV monitor system, revolving stage, and elevators. Air-conditioned; wide, very comfortable seats; no sajiki; orchestra and one balcony in large theater, orchestra only in small theater. Major productions of full-length Kabuki plays occupy the large theater each month, except February and August (Shingeki these months), and in July when young Kabuki actors take important classical roles. Noted for revivals of selected classics; superbly mounted productions; run begins five or six days into the month and continues for twenty-two days. Evening performances weekdays; matinee only on Sundays and national holidays; matinee and evening performances Saturdays.

In the small theater Bunraku has two-week stands; daily performances; different matinee and evening programs. The theater is small, but sit as close as possible to see details of puppet movements, or use opera glasses. It is fascinating to sit far right and have chanter and stage in view at the same time. A kind of Off-Broadway Kabuki can be seen during August; four or five study groups, headed by rising young Kabuki actors, put on programs of classic Kabuki, each program running two or three days. This is genuine Kabuki and what actors lack in experience they more than make up for in youthful vitality. Special festivals of folk theater and dance also play for two- or three-day runs during the summer months. At other times the small theater is rented out. There is no fixed schedule; brief runs often are not advertised; the only sure way is to inquire at the box office or by phone. Both theaters have the same facilities: several restaurants; English-language programs; souvenirs for sale; opera glasses for rent. Interesting theater exhibitions off the mezzanine lobby to the left. Also, the research section mounts educational theater exhibitions on the second floor, which can be reached by entering the business entrance at the back of the theater, then to your left at the top of the stairs.

Kokusai Gekijo (International Theater)***. Two million spectators a year come to see Shochiku Girls' Opera revues at this great barn of a theater set down in the middle of raunchy Asakusa entertainment district. Its scary size (3,270 seats) won't bother you as long as you go first class; sitting in the balcony is like seeing a play from a mountaintop. Built in 1934; no longer glamorous; but seats are comfortable. Eighty-foot wide stage; large side stages; burlesque ramps jut into the auditorium; elaborate stage machinery. Spectacular crashing buildings, waterfalls, moving staircases, and finales marked with fire and steam are standard stage effects. Three incredibly lavish shows a year: Tokyo Dance, end of January until early June; Summer Dance, end of June to early September; and Autumn Dance, September 30 until mid-December. Dark for several weeks between shows. Performances twice a day. Show lasts about 90 minutes and consists of 20–30 fast-paced scenes. More adult and sophisticated than Takarazuka and draws a mixed audience of men and women. Music partly live, partly taped; as unidentifiable as movie music. Cast of 300 girls, technically good dancers; dull choreography, however; no attempt by male impersonators to portray male characteristics (at Takarazuka they do).

Hordes of foreigners come here; English is spoken; restaurant is not recommended; English program, color slides, and 8mm. films of performances for sale in lobby. First-class ticket for foreigners gives you a seat in the first few rows center; or, you can buy an unreserved seat for about a dollar; come in during the movie before the stage show, and grab a seat well down front but on the side. Asakusa is a fascinating district, well worth a whole day of exploring. The theater is near the famous Red Gate (Kaminarimon) entrance to Kannon Temple. Stalls lining the way are crowded at night, but quiet in the afternoon; at one, Gin Kado, you can buy Kabuki properties and dance fans. It's all definitely lowbrow, and like everywhere in Japan it is quite safe.

Meijiza (Meiji Theater)***. A pleasant, medium size, traditional theater; located in an uninteresting mercantile district far from other theaters. In past years Kabuki was staged here; now you see Shimpa, Shinkokugeki, and worthless pickup historical action plays, domestic melodramas, and even revues designed as vehicles for movie stars and popular singers. Primarily female audience; revolving stage and hanamichi; seats 1,743 in narrow seats in orchestra (sajiki along both sides) and two shallow balconies; often sold out to theater parties; restaurants; opera glasses for rent; Japanese programs for sale. This is a good theater, unfortunately being wasted on dull shows. During July you can join Bon groups dancing in Hamacho Park 100 yards to your left as you come out of the theater.

Mokubakan (Mokuba Variety Hall)*. Contains two small and dilapidated variety theaters: first floor, *Naniwabushi*†, hillbilly country singing, and Tabishibai shows; second floor is a Yose. In seedy Asakusa district. Working-class and country audience; seats 200; wooden chairs; air-conditioned; no printed program; unreserved seats.

Nakano Umewaka Gakuin Kaikan (Umewaka School Theater in Nakano)****. An unpretentious and warm Noh stage is contained in this modern (1961) building of concrete and brick. Seats 308 in seven rows, center and left of the stage and in traditional sajiki at rear. Air-conditioned; seats moderately comfortable; though modern, a lovely atmosphere in which to see Noh. Run by the Umewaka branch of the Kanze school. Regular Umewaka-sponsored Noh is given third Sunday morning of the month. Always SRO; be sure to buy in advance or reserve by phone. Other performances several times weekly by amateurs. Rarely open July and August. The theater offers classes to students in Noh singing, acting, drum, and flute; they accept some foreign students in twice-weekly classes.

Nichigeki Mujiku Horu (Nichigeki Music Hall)**. On the fifth floor of the Nihon Gekijo in Yurakucho area. This must be the cleanest nude review in the world. Some men take their wives. Fair dancing; good staging; sharp costuming; some funny sketches. The girls, mostly very pretty, just happen to have most of their clothes off. Music is taped; keyhole stage projects into red velvet-lined auditorium seating 400; a new two-hour show is produced every two months. Audiences are about 10 percent foreigners and 10 percent women; always SRO; Japanese program has two-page English section.

Nihon Gekijo (often abbreviated to **Nichigeki**) (Japan Theater)***. Owned by Toho; conveniently located in Hibiya, in the heart of Yurakucho. Home of Nichigeki Dancing Team since 1935. Like an old Paramount program, you can see a movie and a musical revue on the same bill. Theater is air-conditioned; an ordinary house with orchestra and two balconies; seats 2,614. Three major musical revues are mounted each year using own song-dance troupe—Spring Dance, March–April; Summer Dance, July–August; Autumn Dance, October–November—each lasting 55 days. The same 90-minute show twice a day. Troupe of 80 includes girls and boys, some very sparkling and talented; entirely modern in music and choreography; mostly song and dance, some comedy sketches. Most sophisticated of the musical revue troupes with some fairly interesting dancing. With 10 scenes to Kokusai's 20, there is more time for development; lacks spectacular effects of Kokusai. Some days are sold out to theater parties; call ahead; one English page in program. With first-class ticket you sit center in rows 6–20; or for a small price buy an unreserved seat, come in during the movie and move close to the stage, but on the side. Week-long song and dance shows featuring movie stars and popular singers at other times of the year are a real bore.

Nissei Gekijo (Nissei Theater)****. A luscious sugar-frosting theater in Japan Life Insurance Building; recently built with every conceivable amenity and stage mechanism. Seats 1,353 in orchestra, two-row grand circle (mezzanine), and large balcony. Very comfortable, large seats; restaurants in basement; opera glasses for rent; Japanese program only. Monthly change of bill. A rental theater, mainly used by Shingeki, musical comedy, and prestige foreign troupes. Quality plays in quality productions are the rule.

Shimbashi Embujo (Shimbashi Dance Theater)***. A gem of a little theater much liked by actors for its intimate feeling; hanamichi and revolving stage. An older theater; used for traditional plays; like Kabukiza, owned and operated by Shochiku Company. Located in the Shimbashi geisha district. Between 4:00 and 6:00 P.M. you can still see geisha riding in ricksha to nearby restaurants. Air-conditioned; 1,500 rather narrow seats in an orchestra, with old style sajiki along the sides (favorites with the old-timers, so almost impossible to buy a ticket), and two shallow U-shaped balconies. (I saw my first Kabuki performance here in 1950.) Bill changes monthly: excellent Kabuki each June and sometimes March; Shimpa in January, May, October, and November; Shinkokugeki in February; scores of geisha girls from the Shimbashi district of Tokyo perform in Azuma Odori in April; Zenshinza, a Communist-affiliated troupe which does classic Kabuki as well as Shingeki, in December. Various bills during July, August, and September. Daily matinee and evening programs; 23–25 consecutive days each month. As many as half the performances are sold en bloc to theater parties; reserve by phone or buy in advance. Restaurants; opera glasses for rent; Japanese program.

Shinjuku Bunka (Shinjuku Art Theater)**. An undistinguished movie house that also happens to share its stage with an avant-garde theater troupe after its regular movie showing. Barbara Garson's *Macbird*, LeRoi Jones' (Baraka Imamu's) *Toilet*, and Mishima's modern Noh plays *Yuya* and *Aoi no Ue* have been done here. Usually well performed, using little scenery and much imaginative lighting on a small thrust stage projecting into the 320-seat house. Two-week runs; one performance nightly; no reserved seats; all tickets go on sale 15 minutes before curtain. The line may be long, snaking around the corner into the alley as far as the entrance to the even smaller and more experimental **Theatre Scorpio**, but it moves fast once theater doors are open.

Shinjuku Koma Gekijo ***. An unusual semicircular stage thrusts into the dish-shaped auditorium; large side stages add more width to an already huge stage; special revolving stage is set within a revolving stage; projected film can be background for staged scenes. Seats 2,500 on one floor. House is often sold to theater parties; raucous audiences are often from the country. Musical revues (with taped music), Takarazuka Girls' Opera and Shinkokugeki, trashy action plays, and slapstick farces. Not an important theater but interesting for its stage.

Shinohara Engeijo (Shinohara Variety Theater)*. This is only for the hardy. It is a tiny, ramshackle and hard-to-locate theater for fourth-rate traveling troupes presenting Tabishibai. Like tent shows and Toby shows of the American Midwest in the 1920s and 1930s, ragbag performances for local audiences. The atmosphere is low-down, earthy Japan; spectators talk to performers and put gifts of cigarettes, clothes, and money on stage. Bill has three parts: pseudo-Kabuki historical play in period costume; dance and song interlude (usually dreadful); and a "modern" play. Auditorium is a large room covered with straw matting; small stage; a pathetic attempt at a hanamichi. Troupe changes every two weeks; different play bill nightly; buy ticket at door. Rent a cushion; bring food with you or buy peanuts, beer, sake, there.

Suehirotei (Suehiro Variety Hall)**. Tokyo's most traditional and pleasant Yose for variety programs; in Shinjuku district. Headliners are the top Rakugo storytellers; marvelous audiences; performance every day of the year; up to 18 acts in each four-hour set. Seats 200 in comfortable seats in center and on traditional sajiki along each side; air-conditioned; clean; no advance reservation; buy ticket, unreserved, at the door.

Suidobashi Nohgakudo (Suidobashi Noh Theater)***. An older, highly regarded Noh stage. Seats about 250 in chairs center and on the left side of the auditorium. Traffic noise has now become somewhat distracting. Run by the Hosho school and site of their Noh performances.

Suzumoto Engeijo (Suzumoto Variety Theater)**. A newly built, clean, air-conditioned, comfortable Yose in out-of-the-way Ueno district. Functional and pleasant but lacks Suehiro atmosphere. Seats 300; unreserved seats; variety shows (mostly Rakugo) twice daily.

Takarazuka Gekijo (Takarazuka Theater)****. A large modern theater in Yurakucho district; designed, owned, and run by Toho as the Tokyo home for Takarazuka Girls' Opera. Seats 2,475 in wide, fan-shaped orchestra and two deep balconies; 80-foot proscenium opening; wide side stages; half-moon burlesque rampway projects into audience. Monthly change of program: Girls' Opera in March, April, June, August, September, and November (four troupes rotate during the year); musical comedy—such as *Carousel*—or all-star musicals with performers from all troupes in July and December. One or two performances daily; often sold out to theater parties. Music is live; orchestra is basically Western in style; lavishly costumed and staged; cast of 125 is highly disciplined and attractive. This is the only musical troupe which does musical plays, with dialogue and serious acting. The purity and sweet innocence of Takarazuka should be savored at least once; even if the scripts are dreadful, productions are sparkling and well performed. Audience is 95 percent female; some girls come virtually every day to admire their heroines (and "heroes"). Also "Toho Kabuki" (which is not Kabuki at all), starring the excellent film actor Hasegawa Kazuo (in January and May) and popular dramas starring another superior film actor, Morishige Hisaya (in February and October). With so much else available in Tokyo, there isn't much reason to see these rather ordinary productions, however.

Restaurants; English section in Japanese program; opera glasses (needed in this huge house) and simultaneous translation earphones are for rent in the lobby.

Teikoku Gekijo (or **Teigeki**) (Imperial Theater)****. New; luxuriously appointed; showcase theater in Toho chain. Built in 1966; seats 1,926 in orchestra and one balcony; marvelously comfortable seats; bar in mezzanine and a dozen restaurants in basement; Japanese program occasionally has English section; opera glasses for rent. Usually monthly change of bill; popular plays may run two months or more. Same play given twice daily; Monday and Friday evenings dark. Now what does this superbly equipped theater show? Real Kabuki in December and occasionally musical comedies that are always excellent. Otherwise Toho's "Grand Romances"—perfectly awful marshmallow extravaganzas like *Gone With The Wind*—whose insipidness must be seen to be believed, and tiresome historical melodramas. What a waste. Audience is 70–80 percent female.

Tenjo Sajikikan (Peanut Gallery Theatre)*. Underground theater with a vengeance: a bare basement; audience squats on the floor sharing the tiny 20-foot-square room with the cast. The home theater of Terayama Shuji's brilliant but erratic avant-garde troupe. Wild, participatory, irreverent, ideological, total theater. Productions shock in their all-out assault on society. Short plays lasting an hour or so; open perhaps half the time; no reserved seats so you need to be there by 7:30 for a choice spot to squat; young audience.

Theatro Echo. A tiny, five-row, 100-seat, air-conditioned, bright and utterly charming house; owned by Theatro Echo Shingeki troupe, now in its fifteenth year. Shoes off; actresses serve tea and cookies (free) during intermission; a happy place. Meticulous productions of wittily serious plays, without stars. Two or three productions a year for short runs; always SRO; reserve tickets in advance.

Toho Engeijo (Toho Variety Theater)***. Modern; clean; air-conditioned; comfortable Yose. In Yurakucho; a convenient theater for Rakugo, Kodan, Manzai, juggling, and other variety acts; daily throughout the year (except January 31). A dozen acts on each bill; best performers last. Seats 420; center section reserved; other seats unreserved; cannot reserve in advance; buy at the door.

Toyoko Gekijo (Toyoko Hall)**. A medium-sized, older, long and narrow, one-level theater; rents out to Shingeki, Rakugo, children's plays, and often, in January, Kabuki. Seats 1,002; air-conditioned; Japanese program. An adequate stage, but without machinery. Major productions last three to four weeks and are excellent; minor productions run two or three days and are not particularly recommended.

Yarai Nogakudo (Yarai Noh Theater)***. A tiny, old, wonderfully atmospheric Noh theater. No longer much used. From time to time young performers and even avant-garde groups play here. It is a charming place; only five rows deep; seats 150 in narrow padded chairs center and on the left.

Following is a list of some easy-to-reach places in Tokyo where folk performances are held each year in conjunction with festivals.

Asakusa Kannon Temple, Asakusa Park, Asakusa, Taito-ku. Two unusual ritual folk dances are performed each year in the temple precincts: *Kinryu no Mai,* "Golden Dragon Dance," one day in mid-October (at the same time as the Yasukuni Shrine Autumn Festival), once in the morning and twice in the afternoon; and *Shirasagi no Mai,* "White Stork Dance," an auspicious longevity dance performed November 3 in memory of Emperor Meiji's birthday. To get there see **Kokusai Gekijo**.

Hie Jinja (Hie Shrine), next to the Hilton Hotel, Akasaka, is the site of torchlight Noh each summer. A temporary stage is erected outdoors in the shrine precincts. One or two performances; Friday and/or Saturday in mid-August; advertised in English papers; begins 6:00 P.M. Spotlights pretty much ruin the lovely effect of the firelight. Tightly packed with people; hard folding chairs are crammed on level ground; you can see only if you are lucky enough to get in the first few rows.

Meguro Ginza Street, next to Meguro Station (Yamate surface line), Shinagawa-ku. Everyone joins in dancing Awa Odori, a type of Bon dance, the first Friday and Saturday evenings of August in the blocked-off street. While you're there, try the best deep-fried pork (*tonkatsu*) in town at Tonki, in the station building. Very reasonable.

Meiji Jingu (Meiji Shrine), at Harajuku station (Yamate surface line), Shibuya-ku. Tokyo's chief Shinto shrine with its spacious grounds and pleasant walks is always worth a visit. The site of Tokyo's most impressive outdoor ritual-theater performances: Bugaku court dances, Noh, and Kagura shrine dances are presented on Shinzen Butai, "Outdoor Stage," beside the main shrine during week-long Spring Festival at 11:30 A.M. April 29, 30, and May 2, and at the same hour November 1 and 2 (the two days preceeding Emperor Meiji's birthday) during the Autumn Festival. You can expect tremendous crowds.

Tsukiji Honganji (Tsukiji Buddhist Temple), Tsukiji, Chuoku. Nightly Bon dancing in temple precincts for one week during mid-August. Close to the Ginza and the center of town. Walk one-quarter mile past Kabukiza on Harumidori; temple is on Shin Ohashidori to your left. Or, take Hibiya Subway to Tsukiji station and go out exit in direction of Higashi Ginza.

Ueno Park Zoo, just west of Ueno station, contains an outdoor dancing stage. Edo Dai Kagura, "Great Tokyo Shrine Dance," is performed here at

12:30 P.M. on January 1. Come early; the crowds will be large and the dances do not last long.

Yasukuni Jinja (Yasukuni Shrine), corner of Uchiboridori and Yasu-kunidori, 3-chome, Kudan Ue, Chiyoda-ku. A major site of outdoor perform-ances of traditional performing arts three times a year: New Year Festival, January 1–3; Spring Festival, three days in late April; and Autumn Festival, three days in mid-October. Notices appear in English newspapers. Noh, Kyogen, Kagura, folk dances, Kendo fencing, classical music from 1:00 P.M. No charge. Very easy to find. From Kudanshita station of the Tozai Subway, walk up hill 200 yards; the shrine is to your right at the top. Go through the large gateway on your left and continue until you hear the music. A few rows of benches are set up, but you may have to stand.

Yushima Tenjin Jinja (Yushima Shrine), on Kasugadori, 3-chome, Yushima, Bunkyo-ku, not far from Ueno station. Two festivals are held yearly. Outdoor classical and folk dances can be seen at 1:00 P.M. the first and second Sunday of March. Join Buddhist Bon dancing which goes on nightly for two weeks in late August.

KYOTO. The spirit of old Kyoto is still strong in spite of much modern-ization of the city. The imperial capital of the country for a thousand years, Kyoto is cultivated, placid, and sometimes snobbish. Kabuki began in the bed of the Kamo River, which flows through the city. In the cemetery at the rear of Koto-in Temple at Daitokuji, gravestones mark the resting places of Okuni, the founder of Kabuki, and her partner Nagoya Sanza. Kyoto is famous for its austere Zen temple gardens, but colorful and competing geisha quarters show another side of the city's life. The Pontocho geisha district is a half-mile-long, narrow strip; modern, even flashy, restaurants, bars, and clubs stretch along the west bank of the Kamo River between Shijo and Sanjo bridges. Restaurants on the riverside open onto the still sparkling, clear stream. Though it is marked with a small sign in English, the entrance to narrow Pontocho Lane is so small that it is easy to miss; enter by the police box diagonally across the bridge from the venerable Minamiza theater. At the end of the lane, about 600 yards in, is the **Pontocho Kaburenjo** geisha theater. The Gion geisha district is in the opposite direction. From the Minamiza walk two blocks toward Yasaka Shrine and the eastern hills. Turn right to enter this old-style, subdued entertainment district. You pass ex-cellent restaurants, specialty shops, art stores, teahouses, and candy stores. Gion Corner and the Gion Kaburenjo geisha theater are on your left.

Kyoto's small size and grid-pattern streets make it a comfortable city to get around in. *Kyoto Visitors Map*, published by the Kyoto Association for International Culture and Tourism, Kyoto Grand Hotel, is so good it's worth the effort to find; streetcar lines and stops, temples, restaurants, hotels, and theaters are clearly marked. Kyoto has no subways; recommend taxis or streetcars (system is easy to master with a map, stops are marked in roman letters). Traffic is almost as bad as elsewhere in Japan, but Kyoto is a superb city for walking.

Gion Corner ***. Special performance for tourists, foreign and Japanese, sponsored by the Kyoto City Tourist Association. In a one-hour program see and hear snippets of Bugaku, Bunraku, Kyogen, tea ceremony, Koto music, flower arrangement, and Kyoto-style classical dance. Though brief, each item is carefully and authentically presented. Free English program; performances twice daily, March 1 to November 29.

Gion Kaburenjo (Gion Dance Theater)**. Charming, warm feeling in spite of its 1,300 seats; in a convenient part of town. Air-conditioned; full stage with fly space; hanamichi on both sides of the auditorium; sajiki along the sides of the orchestra and in a U-shape in the balcony add to the atmosphere of old Kyoto. Built as the theater for Gion district geisha dances, *Miyako Odori*†††, staged daily early April through mid-May, and early October through mid-November.

Kongo Nogakudo (Kongo Noh Theater)***. Main theater of the Kongo school of Noh. You enter a long, low passageway in what seems to be an ordinary house. At the end of the passageway you slide open a small door and before you is the Noh theater of your dreams. Ancient, blackened beams support the roof; the stage, a mere foot off the ground and surrounded by pure white crushed rock, seems to float in the air before your eyes; no chairs at all; the whole seating area is sajiki. The passageway for the actors to enter the stage is shorter than usual; the painted pine tree background at the rear of the stage is faded; but this is a magnificent theater for Noh. Most performances weekends; regular Kongo school performances usually fourth Sunday of the month (sometimes third Saturday or third Sunday); starting at noon or later; several full Noh and excerpts (*shimai*) but no Kyogen comedies.

Kyoto Furitsu Bunka Geijitsu Kaikan Horu (Kyoto Municipal Arts Association Hall)***. Well-equipped and extremely attractive new theater; small size (seats 440) and single level design make it pleasant place for intimate drama; wonderfully comfortable seats; air-conditioned. Tickets are inexpensive because most groups using it are small and little known. Rents almost nightly to local dance, music, and Shingeki groups. Monthly schedule of events is printed in Japanese. Art exhibits are shown continuously in two adjoining exhibit halls.

Kyoto Kaikan (Kyoto Hall)***. A beautiful example of modern Japanese architecture; raw concrete and brick exterior, unadorned open interior spaces. Contains two theaters. The large theater (**Dai-ichi Hall**) is a concert hall; no fly space or stage equipment; rents to music, dance, and prestige groups from abroad. Seats 1,300 in orchestra and 500 in balcony; soaring ceiling for warm acoustics. The small theater (**Dai-ni Hall**) is well-equipped; good fly space; side stages; revolving stage; elevators. Seats 810 in orchestra and 240 in shallow balcony. Top Shingeki troupes from Tokyo as well as local amateur troupes play here.

Kyoto Kanze Kaikan (Kyoto Kanze Noh Theater)***. A relatively large, new, warm, and very pleasant Noh theater; conveniently located near Heian Shrine. Seats 600; comfortable seats; three-row balcony; small sajiki section; air-conditioned. Most performances on weekends. Regular Kanze school performances fourth Sunday morning of the month; include four Noh and usually one Kyogen; always SRO; buy tickets in advance. Performances by Noh students some Sunday mornings are free; Noh books are sold in the lobby; theater publishes monthly schedule with some performance dates, hours, and program in English (the month's performances at *all* Noh theaters in Kyoto are included at the back in Japanese).

Minamiza (South Theater)***. Kyoto's only commercial theater; part of the Shochiku chain. A stone beside it reads "On this spot Okuni Kabuki began," commemorating the Shijo crossing of the Kamo River as the site of the first Kabuki performance; a Kabuki theater has stood here ever since. The present building dates from 1929; small in feeling though it seats 1,520; it is old and not much liked by actors. But in my opinion its intimacy and beautifully warm atmosphere make it the finest theater existing in which to see Kabuki. Has traditional revolving stage, traps, hanamichi, and the templelike roof over the stage of early Kabuki theaters. For a feeling of old-style performances, sit on sajiki mats (along both sides of the orchestra and in a U-shape at the front of first and second balconies) as audiences did three hundred years ago. From the first balcony you are only 40 feet from the stage. Bill changes monthly; Kabuki every December is especially good and worth a special trip to Kyoto to see; some years Kabuki also in June and August; always SRO for Kabuki. Popular comedies and traditional singing shows other months.

Oe Nogakudo (Oe Noh Theatre)**. From the street looks like a private house. Performances on weekends only; regular Noh performances are the second Sunday of the month; Kyogen is usually not performed.

Pontocho Kaburenjo (Pontocho Dance Theater)**. An unusual theater that arouses mixed feelings; heavy and squat looking from the outside and built of dirty brick, the Western-style lobby is cramped and cold; inside, the auditorium has a delightfully warm and intimate feeling; only 800 seats. Sitting on sajiki along either side of the orchestra, you are close enough to reach out and touch performers as they pass on the hana-michi. Kyoto-style geisha dance performances, *Kamogawa Odori†††*, are staged twice yearly: mid-April until mid-May, and mid-October until early November.

Important performances are held yearly at shrines and temples in Kyoto.

Arashiyama, near Togetsu-kyo Bridge, is a resort area 10 miles northwest of Kyoto noted for river and mountain scenery. March 10, Noh is performed outdoors at the **Horinji Temple** starting at 1:00 P.M. On November 14 Bugaku court dances and other entertainments are performed as part of the Momiji Matsuri, "Autumn Leaves Festival." By train about 30 minutes from Kyoto. Take the Keifuku Railway, Arashiyama Line, from Shijo Omiya station to Arashiyama station, or the Sannin Main Line, from Kyoto station to Saga station.

Heian Jinja (Heian Shrine), Okazaki, Sakyo-ku, is the site of outdoor performances of torchlight Noh on the nights of June 1 and 2. Excellent performers from Kanze and Kongo schools do four Noh and one Kyogen each night beginning at 5:30 P.M. Chairs are set up on the ground facing the stage; ticket required. Take streetcar No. 22 from downtown to Okazaki Koen Mae stop, walk right two blocks, then left one block.

Mibudera (Mibu Temple), at the western end of Shijodori, Nakagyo-ku. Unique Buddhist comic pantomimes, *Mibu Kyogen††* accompanied by flute, gong, and drums are performed on a stage in the temple grounds every year April 21–30. Possibly the oldest extant form of Japanese theater, dates from 1299; masked cast of about 30 characters; some 20 plays in all. Take taxi.

NAGOYA. Nagoya has no professional theatrical life of its own, but troupes from Tokyo regularly play in the city. Nagoya is relatively small and its roman-letter street signs make it easy to get around in. Theaters are all downtown; taxi fare is low. At the annual Nagoya Matsuri (Nagoya Festival), October 15, you can see performances of folk dances.

Chunichi Gekijo (Chunichi Theater)***. Well-designed, comfortable, new (1967); shallow house; excellent viewing and hearing. Seats 1,500 in orchestra and balcony; air-conditioned; restaurants; Japanese program. Stage is 65 feet wide; equipped with revolving stage. Big Shingeki productions, musical revues, Girls' Opera, and Kabuki all play here; open about half the time; usual run is a few days to a week; matinee and evening performances.

Meitetsu Horu (Meitetsu Hall)***. Another newly built, modern, pleasant theater; seats 900 in steeply raked orchestra, 36 rows deep; air-conditioned; Japanese program for sale. Revolving stage; 50-foot stage. Throughout the year excellent Shingeki troupes use this small theater (*Fantastiks* played here); runs are several days to two weeks.

Misonoza (Misono Theater)***. Nagoya's older, traditional theater; designed with hanamichi and revolving stage for Kabuki; pleasant atmosphere and good acoustics; comfortable; air-conditioned; seats 1,820 in orchestra and rather large balcony. Monthly change of bill; two performances daily. Kabuki is the big attraction each October (and in some years, May); other months, historical dramas by mixed casts of Kabuki actors, movie stars, popular entertainers, and television personalities; also Shinkokugeki, Shimpa, and Zenshinza troupes. Closed last few days of the month.

NARA. Nara was the imperial capital in the eighth and ninth centuries and is called the cradle of Japanese civilization. Sacred and impressive ritual dance and theater performances can be seen: March 13, 9:00 A.M., sacred Shinto dances *Yamatomai,* "Japanese Dance," and *Azuma Asobi,* "Eastern Entertainment," at the main **Kasuga Jinja** (Kasuga Shrine) at the eastern end of Deer Park; May 11 and 12, marvelously atmospheric torchlight Noh, outdoors at **Kofukuji** (Kofuku Temple) at the western end of Deer Park near Sarusawa Pond; November 3, Gagaku court music and Bugaku court dance outdoors in **Manyo Botanical Garden** of Kasuga Shrine; and throughout the day of December 17 at **Kasuga Wakamiya Jinja** (just south of the main Kasuga Shrine) Kagura sacred dances, and celebratory Noh and Kyogen plays honoring the gods are performed outdoors in front of the shrine entrance. The Kasuga Wakamiya performances are part of Nara's largest festival, the On Matsuri, which draws throngs of Japanese and foreign tourists, especially to see the colorful procession of people dressed as warriors and nobles. Nara is one hour by express train from Kyoto or Osaka.

OSAKA. Japan's second largest city, a business and trade center, Osaka has always had a special atmosphere. In many ways it is a huge, overgrown country town. The nature of the Osaka spirit is not easy to describe, but it tends to sentimentality and simple humor. Tokyo, the center of samurai government for three hundred years, venerated the warrior spirit; Osaka is a commoner's and a merchant's town. Chikamatsu wrote Bunraku plays about tragic young Osaka townsmen and women in the eighteenth century. The most characteristic Osaka drama of today is *Shochiku Shinkigeki*††, (Shochiku New Comedy); simple, TV situation-drama placed on stage. Its marvelously facile star and comic Fujiyama Kammi, is Harold Lloyd, Slim Pickens, and Rochester rolled into one. There are slick new theaters for commercial entertainments scattered about town, but the old and famous entertainment district is Dotombori, where since the seventeenth century Kabuki and Bunraku theaters have been side-by-side; this is a very small area and marvelous for walking; closed to cars. Another group of theaters is clustered in the north around Umeda station.

Asahiza (Asahi Theater)***. Dotombori. This intimate and well-kept theater is the home of Bunraku puppet-theater in Japan today. Its relatively small size (990 seats), hanamichi, and right side-stage for puppet musicians and chanters, are designed for Bunraku; air-conditioned; sajiki along sides of orchestra for relaxed seating. Bunraku plays four times a year for two weeks, usually January, April, July–August, and September–October. Two different bills each day; in summer one bill a day; English section in Japanese program; theater is seldom sold out; can buy ticket at door. Small folk-song, dance, and Shingeki groups rent theater at other times. Packed together along Dotombori are three theaters and two cinemas, in order: Shochiku Cinema, Nakaza, Kadoza, Toei Cinema, and finally Asahiza, There are dozens of bars and restaurants specializing in seafood and small kabobs (*kushi katsu*); a maze of retail stalls is just across the river.

Festibaru Horu (Festival Hall)****. Osaka's entry in the competition to build Japan's largest and best theater. Built in 1958 by the *Asahi* newspaper, it looks like new. Stage is really too large; 100 feet wide; has 16 electric elevators and traps, sliding stages, and side-stages for entries. Seats 2,980 in orchestra (steeply raked second half) and balcony (called "gallery"); house is 80 seats across. Highest priced tickets in Japan; boxes, most expensive seats of all, are 15 rows back in orchestra and a bad deal; your best buy is first few rows of the balcony; rent opera glasses. Prestigious Osaka International Festival, sponsored by the Osaka *Asahi*, is held here yearly in April and May; your travel agent will have information; usually SRO; buy tickets well in advance. Other foreign groups perform during the year, as well.

Kadoza (Corner Theater)**. In Dotombori entertainment district. For more than two hundred years the name Kadoza meant one of Osaka's major Kabuki theaters. No longer used for traditional plays, the Kadoza now is one of Osaka's five Yose, or variety halls. Seats 1,008; comfortable; air-conditioned; seldom crowded; no reserved seats. A ticket is good all day. Dark only one or two days a year; Japanese program; 13–14 typically boisterous, rural-flavored Osaka-style acts (routines last up to half an hour or 40 minutes, longer than in Tokyo Yose); includes Osaka-style vaudeville duos (*Manzai*), traditional countryside narrative singing (*Naniwabushi*), modern storytelling (*Mandan*†), juggling, Chinese comic magicians, virtuoso shamisen playing, and popular vocalistics. Traditional comic Rakugo is less popular than in Tokyo. A Shochiku theater.

Nakaza (Middle Theater)**. One of Osaka's older theaters; in Dotombori; recommended for its traditional atmosphere. Has hanamichi, revolving stage, and traps for Kabuki. Audience eats lunch in theater; sit in sajiki section on either side of orchestra or in front of balcony for delightful place to watch play and audience. Seats 1,030; air-conditioned; rather narrow seats; some performances sold out to theater parties. A Shochiku theater and home of Shochiku Shinkigeki performances seven months a year. Similar troupes play most other months. Sometimes in July or August plays Kabuki. Closed the first few days of each month. In the West we no longer have live drama about average people; Shinkigeki dramatizes the lives of the lower-middle and working class. Acting is often extremely skilful; the plays are hack pieces. Two bills a day of three plays each.

Shin Kabukiza (New Kabuki Theater)****. Shochiku's new theater in Osaka for traditional drama. Plush with all the frills; very comfortable seating for 1,883 in orchestra and two balconies; sajiki seating along sides of orchestra; air-conditioned; hanamichi; sliding wagons instead of revolving stage. Monthly change of bill; dark last days of the month; traditional Kabuki, featuring Osaka-style plays, in May (and, some years, in January or February and April as well). Other than this, the theater is wasted on styleless historical romances featuring Shochiku movie stars, complete with taped movie music and purple spots; highly avoidable fare; largely female audience. A problem with this theater is that tickets are expensive and that all the orchestra and first balcony are first-class seats; cheaper tickets only for the second balcony.

Takarazuka Dai Gekijo (Takarazuka Grand Theater)***. A Toho theater. In 1911 when Hankyu Railway built a line to the spa of Takarazuka outside Osaka, it also built a theater and formed Japan's first Girls' Opera troupe as an attraction to get people to ride its trains. Four Takarazuka troupes (Moon, Sun, Star, Flower) alternate monthly programs in this theater, in Tokyo, and in other cities. A training school for new members is attached. Takarazuka was the subject of the movie *Sayonara*. Theater is located within Takarazuka Park, which has zoo, rides, monorail, baths. The theater is not particularly impressive; it is large (seats 3,000 in orchestra and two balconies); tickets are very cheap. Foreign visitors often come here; several restaurants (expensive); English program for sale; can rent opera glasses or earphones for simultaneous translation. Audience is mostly teenage girls. Disregard your program's claim that Takarazuka is the "center of entertainment in Japan"; it is a pleasant, pretty, and bright musical show but not more. Strangely, the Western part of the bill is stronger than the traditional Japanese dance part. I don't think this is worth the half hour trip. Performances are same as at Takarazukaza in Tokyo and the Tokyo theater is more congenial. Near the main theater is a smaller house, **Shingeki Gekijo** (Modern Drama Theater)**, where rather uninteresting modern plays are staged every other month. There are hotels and Japanese inns for overnight stay.

Umeda Koma Gekijo**. A Toho theater. The circular stage is a twin of Koma Gekijo in Tokyo. A barn of a place, seating 2,400 in orchestra and balcony; comfortable seats; air-conditioned. Has 50-girl dancing team that works with Toho movie stars in second-rate musical revues and Milton Berle comedy sketches. Sometimes pop and rock shows. Bill changes five, six times a month; young audience.

REGIONAL PERFORMANCES

CHICHIBU CITY,   Saitama Prefecture. December 1–3, elaborately decorated floats constructed like Kabuki sets are pulled to various places in the city. Local performers do traditional Kabuki plays on the floats for audiences standing in the streets. As Chichibu is 65 miles north of Tokyo, this is the most convenient regional Kabuki to try to see. Also, **Chichibu Jinja** (Chichibu Shrine) is famous for its sacred Kagura shrine dance performed December 3, and on other occasions.

CHUSONJI.   In the countryside near Hiraizumi, southern Iwate Prefecture. Founded by the Fujiwara family in 1105, the temple was for centuries an outpost in the north of ancient Heian culture. Rarely seen *Ennen* Buddhist longevity dances and Noh plays are performed in antiquated style each May on a lone and rustic Noh stage set in the midst of a pine grove. About 60 miles north of Sendai, Tohoku main line.

GOKOKU JINJA (Gokoku Shrine), Hikone City, Shiga Prefecture. Torchlight Noh from 5:00 P.M. October 29 as part of Shiro Matsuri (Castle Festival), October 24–November 3. Hikone is on Lake Biwa, between Nagoya and Kyoto, on the Tokaido line.

ISE JINGU (Ise Grand Shrine). The main Shinto shrine in Japan. Ancient ritual Kagura dances honor deities during Ise Jingu Kagura Sai (Ise Shrine Kagura Festival), April 5–7, at the dance halls of both of the Inner and Outer Shrines (they are 4 miles apart). The Outer Shrine (Geku) is easiest to reach: after a few minutes walk from Uji-Yamada station, cross the bridge in front of the first torii, and continue on to the second one where the Kagura Hall (Kaguraden) is located. Ise is about two hours by train from Nagoya or Osaka.

ITSUKUSHIMA JINJA (Itsukushima Shrine). On the island of Itsukushima (or Miyajima); famous for being built over the Inland Sea, so that the shrine buildings appear to float on the water. Kagura and Bugaku court dances can be commissioned for a fee. They are performed on dance stages overlooking the sea; in the background a great cyprus torii rises from the water. Bugaku is performed on decorated boats that are towed from the shrine across the channel to the mainland during Kangensai (Court Music Festival), in mid-July. Offertory Noh and Kyogen, April 16–18, is a never-to-be-forgotten spectacle: the audience seated on the shore looks across a stretch of water at the day-long performances on the over-water Noh stage. Itsukushima is 20 miles south of Hiroshima on the Sanyo main line; at Miyajimaguchi station take ferry boat to the island.

KAMAKURAGU (Kamakura Shrine), Kamakura City. Torchlight Noh is performed on an outdoor stage two consecutive evenings in late September beginning at 5:00 P.M. Kamakura City is an hour by train from Tokyo; the shrine is one mile northeast of Kamakura station.

KOSAIJI (Kosai Temple), Mushio Village, Hikari-machi, Sosa-gun, Chiba Prefecture. Villagers give a single performance in mid-July of *Kiraigo*, "Masked Demon Play"; a remnant of medieval Buddhist morality plays (*Nembutsu Kyogen*) in which the Bodhisattva Jizo saves the dead from tortures inflicted by demons in hell. A one-day trip from Tokyo. Ask JTB for travel help.

KUROMORI HIE SHRINE, Kuromori Village, Sakata City, Yamagata Prefecture. Each February 15 farmers of the village perform traditional Kabuki plays during the day on a stage built in the shrine grounds. The audience sits in the open on mats spread on the snow-covered ground. At least a two-day trip going and coming to this very cold area in northern Honshu. Ask JTB for travel help.

NAGAHAMA CITY, Shiga Prefecture. April 10–17 floats are pulled through the streets; on each float local casts perform scenes of archaic Kabuki (the style dates back to the 1760s). The city was the center of the sixteenth-century fief of the Regent Toyotomi Hideyoshi, and the festival is said to have begun in that century to honor the birth of his son. Nagahama is on the shore of Lake Biwa, midway between Nagoya and Kyoto, ten minutes on the Hokuriku line from Maibara.

SUWA JINJA (Suwa Shrine), Nagasaki City. October 7–9, Okunchi Matsuri, or Suwa Shrine Festival, features dances of Chinese origin during a grand parade that passes by the broad steps of the shrine each afternoon. The festival celebrates Nagasaki's long history of contact with China. Nagasaki is on the west coast of Kyushu.

TOKUSHIMA CITY, Tokushima Prefecture. The most incredible Bon dances in Japan are here. Upwards of one and a half million people come to see 400 groups dance the Awa Odori through the streets of the city day and night for four consecutive days, August 15–18. Everyone joins in; it's like Carnival or Mardi Gras. So popular with tourists (foreign and Japanese) that JTB runs special tours to Tokushima during the festival. Tokushima is on the island of Shikoku, a long day's trip from Tokyo.

Books to Read

GENERAL: Tsuruo Ando, *Bunraku* (New York: Walker/Weatherhill, 1970); Peter D. Arnott, *The Theatres of Japan* (New York: St. Martin's Press, 1969); Faubion Bowers, *Japanese Theatre* (New York: Hill and Wang, 1959); Earle Ernst, *The Kabuki Theatre* (Honolulu: University Press of Hawaii, 1974); Masakatsu Gunji, *Kabuki* (Palo Alto, Calif.: Kodansha International, 1969); Aubrey and Giovanna Halford, *The Kabuki Handbook* (Rutland, Vt.: Charles E. Tuttle, 1966); Donald Keene, *No: The Classical Theatre of Japan* (Palo Alto, Calif.: Kodansha International, 1966), and *Bunraku: The Art of the Japanese Puppet Theatre* (Palo Alto, Calif.: Kodansha International, 1965); Donald Kenney, *A Guide to Kyogen* (Tokyo: Hinoki Shoten, 1968); Yasuo Nakamura, *Noh: The Classical Theater* (New York: Walker/Weatherhill, 1971); P. G. O'Neill, *A Guide to Noh* (Tokyo: Hinoki Shoten, 1953); J. Thomas Rimer, *Toward a Modern Japanese Theatre: Kishida Kunio* (Princeton, N.J.: Princeton University Press, 1974); Seami, *Kadensho* (Kyoto: Sumiya-Shinobe, 1968).

PLAYS: Kobe Abe, *Friends* (New York: Grove Press, 1969); James R. Brandon, *Kabuki: Five Classic Plays* (Cambridge, Mass.: Harvard University Press, 1975), and with Tamako Niwa, *Kabuki Plays: Kanjincho and The Zen Substitute* (New York: Samuel French, 1966); Shusaku Endo, *The Golden Country* (Rutland, Vt.: Charles E. Tuttle, 1966); Earle Ernst, ed., *Three Japanese Plays from the Traditional Theatre* (London: Oxford University Press, 1969); Mokuami Kawatake, *The Love of Izayoi and Seishin* (Rutland, Vt.: Charles E. Tuttle, 1966); Donald Keene,*Chushingura: The Treasury of Loyal Retainers* (New York: Columbia University Press, 1971), *Major Plays of Chikamatsu* (New York: Columbia University Press, 1961), and *Twenty Plays of the No Theatre* (New York: Columbia University Press, 1970); Kokusai Bunka Shinkokai, *The Noh Drama* (Rutland, Vt.: Charles E. Tuttle, 1960); Richard McKinnon, *Selected Plays of Kyogen* (Tokyo: Uniprint, 1968); Yukio Mishima, *Five Modern Noh Plays* (New York: Alfred A. Knopf, 1957), and *Madame de Sade* (New York: Grove Press, 1967); Shio Sakanishi, *Japanese Folk Plays* (Rutland, Vt.: Charles E. Tuttle, 1960); Makoto Ueda, *The Old Pine Tree* and *Other Noh Plays* (Lincoln, Neb.: University of Nebraska Press, 1962).

Korea

Korea's geographic position has meant that for centuries Chinese culture and arts have influenced those of Korea. In turn, Koreans introduced performing arts of the continent to the Japanese. Today, Korea's ancient court-music and dance traditions are maintained and performed with considerable vigor; court theatrical forms—the masked dance-drama in particular—unfortunately are preserved only in remnants and we can do no more than guess at their splendor in the past. Unless you are interested primarily in modern drama, the amount of theater you might see in Korea is probably not sufficient to plan a special theater trip to this otherwise dynamic and interesting country. At the same time, it is striking how highly Koreans themselves value theater art. Korea was the first country in Asia to establish a viable National Theater and to provide regular financial support for the performing arts. And folk theater—storytelling narratives, masked plays, and puppet-plays—all have a long and vital history. Government censorship is all-pervasive, stifling any political thought through drama; in spite of this, modern drama is pursued with intense seriousness and vitality by many talented writers and performers. Theatrical study and research groups and institutes are extremely active.

Seoul is very much the theatrical center of the country. Major theatrical traditions are national, and hence available as much in Seoul as elsewhere. Unless you wish to see special performances in villages, there is no need to travel from one region to another to see what Korea offers in drama. Performances are sponsored, as a rule, by permanent groups; the troupe system adds an element of continuity to the theater scene.

THEATERGOING

Seoul's few theaters range from excellent to adequate. The best troupes are semiprofessional. A troupe will mount three or four productions a year, for runs of a week or so. At best you might be able to see two or three plays during a week's stay. Curtain time is 7:30 P.M. There is no central ticket-selling agency; buy at the theater; tickets are inexpensive.

SEASON. Theaters in the city are in use through most of the year except in July or August. The summer's heat is so oppressive that theater comes to a stop everywhere in the country.

FESTIVALS. Important religious festivals occur on: New Year's, during the full moon of the first lunar month (February); Buddha's birthday on the eighth day of the fourth month (May); the fifth day of the fifth lunar month (June), called Tano, the Swing Festival; and the Harvest Festival, on the full moon of the eighth lunar month (September). In villages in many parts of Korea you can see music, dance, and drama performed as part of these festivals.

TRANSPORTATION. It is easy to travel between major cities in Korea by air, train, or express bus. Seoul is too large to walk to most theaters; only an occasional street sign is in roman letters. Take taxis; they are metered, inexpensive, can be hailed on the street.

INFORMATION. Daily English-language newspapers list some, but not all, performances in Seoul: see "Calendar" in the *Korea Herald* and "Town Crier" in the *Korea Times*. Otherwise, check theaters directly to see what is playing.

WHAT TO SEE

Ceremonial court music and dance go back a thousand years; they are preserved in superb concerts of the National Classical Music Institute. Sounds are ethereal; dance is stately and grand; historically and stylistically related to Bugaku in Japan. A concert consists of several unconnected musical and dance numbers. *Keum-mu* ††† is a vigorous sword dance of a fifteen-year-old hero; *Kugo-mu* †††, "Nine Drum Dance," is a descendent of Buddhist rituals in which the performer dances while beating an intricate rhythm on nine drums of different sizes and pitches; the *Fan Dance* †† was brought to Korea from China, perhaps in the seventh century; the *Wedding Dance* †† is a sophisticated version of a former folk dance. (Theater: Kulip Kukjang.)

Sandae†† (or †††) are masked dances going back many centuries. Troupes were attached to the royal court in Seoul and were summoned to perform for important Buddhist ceremonial occasions and for the entertainment of

Chinese imperial envoys. In the seventeenth century when court support ceased, performers formed wandering troupes and scattered through the countryside to earn their livings. Their descendents preserve, in folk form, in different parts of the country, masked dance-plays that are remarkably similar to each other. Villages where the forms are known today are in Kosong, Tongyong, and Tongrae in the south; at Yangju a few miles north of Seoul; and at Kangnung on the east coast. December, January, and June (the Tano Festival) are the best times to see masked dances in these villages. Private dance schools and the National Classical Music Institute teach the masked dance-play to students; excerpts are sometimes included in dance recitals in

Farmers of Yangju, Korea, perform a masked-play in the outer yard of the local temple. Masked and dressed in white, the Young Monk begins the drama.

Seoul. The traditional masked dance-play is acted only by men; simple but colorful costumes are worn; drums, oboe, and fiddle accompany high-stepping and often lively, whirling dance movements; pantomime is limited; dialogue and chanting by the characters alternate with dance.

Masks of the *Yangju Sandae* dance-play†† are dish-shaped disks of gourd, with stylized slashes for eyes and eyebrows, red circles for the painted cheeks of a courtesan, and round dots for a monk's boils. Elegantly carved wooden masks were worn in times past when the masked play was performed in the Hahoe district; examples of these beautiful masks can be seen in the National Museum, Seoul. Paper masks worn in the *Pongsan Sandae* dance-play†† were burned after use; spirits residing in the masks would make them dangerous to be kept near at hand. Wherever the masked play is seen, it consists of 10–15 scenes on more or less the same topics: Buddhist monks squabble over a courtesan's affections; a country noble is satirized; a lovely young female shaman tempts an old priest to break his vow of celibacy; a monkey leaps and dances to ridicule another monk; a husband and wife quarrel. A play begins with a ceremonial offering to the spirits of the locale and to the masks; it ends with a Buddhist service for the wife in the play who has died. In courts in the past it undoubtedly was a sophisticated dance-play; in villages today it is a simple folk performance, mixing rudimentary dance with bawdy verbal humor that its country audience loves.

Pansori ††† is a danced and acted-out narrative tale, performed by one woman. In the eighteenth century, twelve lengthy stories were in the Pansori repertory; today five of these are known and performed. What does the solo actor-dancer do? The story is composed of songs, which she sings and dances simultaneously, and of dialogue, which she speaks, playing one after the other all the roles in the story. A drummer provides a steady beat during the dance and punctuates important dialogue with sharp drum phrases. Pansori is an extremely demanding art form, blending feminine grace with powerful delivery. It began as a folk art in Cholla Province in the southwest; most performers today are from that area. Your best chance to see and hear Pansori would be a concert performance in Seoul; in celebration of the Harvest Festival, during the full moon of the eighth lunar month (September), a special performance is given at the Kulip Kukjang theater. Recommended regional performance at Namwon.

Changkuk †† is Pansori theatricalized—actresses and actors taking roles, scenery marking locales, and the whole being presented in a theater as a kind of grand opera. Or rather, it was, for Changkuk was widely popular among the urban middle-class audience 40–50 years ago. It hasn't been staged regularly for years. Should you chance on a revival, don't miss it.

Itinerant professional players have performed glove-puppet plays, *Kkoktu*

Kaksi†, in Korean villages for many centuries. A chief puppeteer manipulates two puppets, one on each hand, over his head; he speaks the dialogue of main characters. A "speaker" in the orchestra (gong, oboe, drums, and fiddle) takes the voices of minor characters; on either side of the small stage a puppet assistant moves puppets on and off. The single play which is performed recounts follies of the nobility, ridicules venial and corrupt monks, and satirizes marital problems. It is similar to the play of the masked dance-drama and the two forms are certainly related. Kkoktu Kaksi is a simple folk art, attuned to its village audience. Boisterous action and earthy, satirical humor are its strong points. Once performed all over Korea, a handful of puppeteers remains today. Not easy to find a performance.

Modern drama, or *Singkuk*††, is the liveliest of Korea's dramatic forms. Korean students studying in Tokyo performed their first translations of Western plays in 1908. Early productions were mostly topical melodramas, like Japanese Shimpa; after the 1920s a wide audience was built up for serious, intellectual drama, similar to the Japanese style of Shingeki and in part influenced by it. Strong interest in modern drama led in 1950 to the building in downtown Seoul of a National Theater (Kulip Kukjang) that provided a home for partially subsidized, semiprofessional resident dance, music, and drama companies. Today, this theater, now called the Yesul Kukjang, rents to independent theater groups. In 1973 a new Kulip Kukjang, containing a large and a small theater, was constructed; it took over the function of housing nationally subsidized and resident companies. There are also about ten well-known Singkuk drama troupes that are independent and not affiliated with the Kulip Kukjang. Important ones are: Dong Nanang (Drama Centre of Korea), Silhom (Experiment), Kwangjang (Echo), Jayu (Freedom), Shinhyup (Reform). Though not fully professional, they present well-staged productions ranging from Shakespeare and Greek tragedy in Korean translation to avant-garde experiments by young playwrights like Tae-suk Oh and directors like Deuk-hyong Yoo. (Theaters: Kulip Kukjang, Drama Centre, Cafe Theatre, Yesul Kukjang.)

WHERE TO GO

SEOUL. In addition to the theaters listed below, several new theaters are currently being planned or are under construction, and should open in 1976 or 1977: to replace the municipal theater that was destroyed by fire in 1972 a new 2,000-seat City Hall is under construction; being completed by the Korean Culture and Arts Foundation is a People's Theater, seating 150, for which contemporary Korean plays will be commissioned for production by major Singkuk groups. Also being planned for downtown is a 150-seat theater for the Ejato Company and a 200-seat theater for the Silhum Company.

Cafe Theatre**. A delightful coffee house where avant-garde plays, often one-acters, are imaginatively staged. Performances normally Tuesday and Friday, but schedule is irregular; never on weekends; check by phone before you go. A play runs a month or so; sometimes two plays in repertory; home of Jayu troupe; also rents to other groups. Seats 150 at tables in large room; no one is farther than 20 feet from minuscule platform-stage set in corner; air-conditioned; your ticket includes hot tea. This is a student rendezvous in the middle of active restaurant and bar area. Sharply managed; attentive service; sparkles with vitality. Highly recommended.

Drama Centre***. Like a small Greek amphitheater; exceptionally well-designed; imaginative; built in 1962. Seats 500 in 10 semicircular, steeply-stepped rows; comfortable seats; air-conditioned. Four aisles leading down into the half-round thrust stage can be used for performance entrances and exits; open foyer at top of aisles and behind audience can become a "choir stage"; a tunnel connects dressing rooms beneath stage with forestage, allowing players to suddenly appear in view. Here is total flexibility, a play occurring in front of, behind, above, around, and beneath the audience. Home of the Drama Centre troupe; also occasionally rents to other modern drama groups. A production runs one to two weeks; four or five productions a year; phone for schedule. Attached to the theater is the Korean Institute for Theatre Research, Seoul School of Drama (two-year professional course), and theater library.

Korea House***. Run by Ministry of Culture and Information for visitors. Performances of court and folk dance are staged free of charge Saturday and Sunday through the year, plus Tuesday and Thursday during March–June and September–October. The stage is the polished wooden floor of a large room in a traditional mansion. You sit informally on cushions in adjoining rooms. During warm weather doors are slid open on a beautiful surrounding garden and fishpond. Accomodates only 150; very popular and crowded; come a little early to get a good place to sit. Easy to find; cameras are permitted; English is spoken by everyone; English program free of charge. Adjoining restaurant serves Korean food before performance, is closed when performance is over. Several private classical-dance schools provide students to perform; a bill of six or seven dances lasts an hour. Drum Dance is exciting; Wedding Dance done by five-year olds is overly cute; performers are moderately skilled and most dances are genuinely presented. This is an easy way to get a taste of Korean classical and folk dance.

Kulip Kukjang (National Theater)****. A handsome new building perched on a tree-clad hill in Seoul's outskirts. Dedicated in 1973; contains two air-conditioned theaters; both are beautiful. The **Tai Kukjang**, "large theater," seats 1,494 in broad, gently-raked orchestra, a four-row royal circle, and a large balcony. Huge stage, as large as the auditorium, is equipped with revolving stage, elevator, wagons, and 100-foot flies. The **Soo Kukjang**, "small theater," seats 344 on single level; stage is modestly proportioned; half-flies; excellent viewing and acoustics. Program is printed in Korean, sometimes also in English. Eight resident troupes are attached to the theater and use its facilities for rehearsal and performance: modern drama, Western symphony orchestra, Western ballet, Western opera, Western musicals, chorus, Korean traditional music and dance, and Pansori. Other groups can rent when theaters are empty. Adjoining buildings, also new, house the National Classical Music Institute and offices of performing groups.

Yesul Kukjang (formerly old Kulip Kukjang)***. Opened just before the Korean War began in 1950; now replaced by the new national theater just described. A warm, comfortable, relaxing house; beautiful acoustics; although it is fairly large (seats 1,100) it seems small; balcony is wonderfully close and I recommend sitting there; seats are narrow; stage is adequately equipped. Demand for theaters in Seoul is great and this theater rents constantly to modern drama groups; matinee and evening performances each day of a run.

REGIONAL PERFORMANCES

KANGNUNG, Kangwon Province. A remarkable week-long festival of ancient, pre-Buddhist, shaman ritual dances coincides with the Tano Festival in June. Kangnung city is 150 miles from Seoul on the eastern sea coast.

NAMWON, Cholla Province. The finest Pansori singers in the area converge on Namwon during the Chunhyan Festival (fifth day of the fifth lunar month). Continuous performances for two or three days. Namwon city is 250 miles south of Seoul.

Books to Read

Sang-su Choe, *A Study of the Korean Puppet Play* (Seoul: Korea Books, 1961); Duhyon Lee, *Korean Mask-Dance Drama* (Seoul: Ministry of Culture and Information, 1969); In-sob Zong, *Plays from Korea* (Seoul: Chang-an University, 1968).

Laos

With a population of about three million, Laos is one of the smallest countries in Asia. North and east of Thailand, it has always been off the beaten track for travelers. In recent years only a few hardy souls take the overland trip through northeast Thailand to Vientiane, on the northern bank of the Mekong River. Others fly there from Bangkok, or to the inland capital of Luang Prabang. Though these are Laos' two major cities, they are small, quiet provincial towns.

Three styles of drama are performed in Laos: classical dance and dance scenes—virtually identical to those seen in Thailand or in Cambodia (although on a smaller scale); ribald courting jousts sung to Laotian folk music; and a Lao version of Thai popular drama. Theater is not easy to find in Laos and few people will want to make a special trip to this out-of-the-way area just for theater.

THEATERGOING

Major places to look for classical dance, in the event you are in Laos, are at the National School of Music and Dance (Natasin School) in Vientiane or, in Luang Prabang, at the grand palace. Classical performances are rare, but if you should hear of one you can ask to see it. Popular dramas are staged in ramshackle commercial theaters, built of bamboo and thatch, usually dirt floored, hot, and uncomfortable, or in the open air at temple festivals with folding chairs simply set up on the grass. Performance begins at 8:00 or 9:00 P.M. and continues past midnight.

SEASON.   There is no season for classical dance; a performance is given on command of the government, for state and other special occasions, and there are other more or less public performances from time to time. July–August is the wet season when nothing is seen. The best time for weather and for theater is October–December, the dry, cool season.

FESTIVALS.   During the dry season, Buddhist temples all over Laos hold temple fairs (*wat boun*); one or two troupes will always be playing at a fair. Chief temple fair in Vientiane is at **Wat Dong Mieng**; three or four days in late November.

TRANSPORTATION.   You can fly to Vientiane and Luang Prabang from Bangkok. Within cities there is no public transportation; cars can be hired at hotels.

INFORMATION.   Tourists are rare in Laos. There is no good published source of information on theater. Try asking your hotel clerk and taxi drivers.

WHAT TO SEE

Cambodian classical dance and dance scenes were introduced into Laos in 1353, when Prince Fa Nguan left the Cambodian capital of Angkor to establish an independent Lao kingdom. He built his capital at Luang Prabang. Since that time the Lao court has supported a classical music and dance troupe to provide entertainment at religious and state functions. The royal troupe today consists of 90 dancers, musicians, singers, and teachers, divided between the king's court in Luang Prabang and the government's Natasin School of Music and Dance (also called the University of Fine Arts) in Vientiane. In costuming, staging, music, and dance vocabulary, it is the same art as is practiced in Cambodia and Thailand. In fact, advanced Lao dancers go to Bangkok for further training. Female dance predominates; male masked dance, while known, is seldom performed. With the limited resources of the small Lao court lengthy dance-dramas cannot be staged; the usual performance is a dance concert consisting of separate, short dance items.

Mohlam†† is a distinctively Lao art. It is a style of singing. Accompanied by a musician playing a Lao reed panpipe (*khen*), that sounds something like a small organ, a singer races through verbally elaborate verses, one after the other, that titillate through erotic suggestion and hyperbole, comment upon local events of interest, and offer philosophic homilies. Mohlam is immensely popular among villages where Lao is spoken: in Laos proper and in northeast Thailand, just across the border, where the bulk of the population is ethnically and linguistically Lao. Hundreds of Mohlam teams wander from village to village carrying on their traditional entertainment and newsgiving function.

Female court dancers in Laos performing male and female roles in a sophisticated version of a folk dance-play. (Photo courtesy Royal Lao Department of Culture.)

Mohlam Luong†, "story Mohlam," is a hybrid play form performed in commercial theaters in all parts of Laos. In the early part of this century Likay troupes (see **Thailand**) came across the Mekong River from the south into Laos. Audiences liked the plays, so local singers and musicians put them to Mohlam music. Mohlam Luong is the result: local history and legendary stories performed in Mohlam musical style. About 80 percent song, 20 percent spoken dialogue. Troupes consist of 15–20 performers; about 40 troupes move from theater to theater in Laos and in northeast Thailand. The level of acting is not very high, although the lead comic is often skilful. The music and singing style is intricate and may remind you of a fugue; the stamina of the performers is astonishing. Mohlam Luong is also called *Mohlam Mu*, "group Mohlam," *Lam Mu*, "group singing," or *Lam Luong*, "sung story."

WHERE TO GO

Inquire at the **Natasin School of Music and Dance** in Vientiane about a possible performance of classical dance; you will need an invitation to attend. Usually one or two Mohlam Luong troupes are performing in Vientiane and in Luang Prabang. Unfortunately they move about and only a person on the spot can say where a troupe might be playing; often a troupe plays near **Wat Khounta**, a Buddhist temple, by Vientiane airport. Temple festivals are major events of the year; anyone you ask should know if an important festival is under way.

Book to Read

James R. Brandon, *Theatre in Southeast Asia* (Cambridge, Mass.: Harvard University Press, 1967).

Malaysia

Standing across the trade routes linking China on the east and India and the Arab countries to the west, the Malay Peninsula has for centuries been a meeting ground for various cultures. Ethnically the population is Malay and Chinese in about equal numbers, with a small minority of East Indian descent. Cultural influence from Malaysia's neighbors, Thailand and Indonesia, is strong. Finally, there were the British. Theater in Malaysia reflects its diverse cultural heritages. At certain times and places, you can see Malay traditional dance-plays and shadow-drama, Indian classical dancing, Chinese opera and puppet plays, Thai influenced dance-drama, and Western-style modern drama.

Nonetheless, Malaysia is not a cosmopolitan country; its traditional and even much of its modern theater are strongly rooted in folk culture. Performances in the countryside are charmingly casual. Variety of forms is Malaysia's dramatic strong point. The amount of theatrical activity can easily be underestimated because professional urban theater does not exist, and performances by the hundreds of shadow-play puppeteers and the scores of traditional dance-drama troupes in remote country areas in the north pass unnoticed.

THEATERGOING

A handful of urban theaters exists in Malaysia's two major cities, Kuala Lumpur and Penang. Several are newly built, modern, and comfortable for spectators; most have poorly equipped stages. The great majority of performances take place in the countryside, either in the open or in temporary theaters made of bamboo and palm thatch.

SEASON. Malaysia is a tropical country, situated just above the equator; the weather is hot, but not oppressive. Between December and February torrential rains fall in the northeastern part of the peninsula making shadow-play and dance-drama performances impossible. The best time to find shadow-plays, especially in Kelantan State, is in April, during the dry season.

FESTIVALS. Planning your visit to coincide with a festival is a good way to find traditional performances within urban surroundings. All through the year, plays of many kinds are staged during national celebrations and Islamic and Buddhist festivals. State holidays, usually celebrating the birthday of the state ruler or chief executive, are particularly rich occasions for seeing theater in provincial towns. Free performances of all kinds are staged at Panggong Anniversary, Lake Gardens, Kuala Lumpur, on August 31, Hari Kabangsaan Malaysia, or National Day of Malaysia, and the night following. At the end of Buddhist Lent (October) look for Thai-style shadow-plays and Menora dance-plays in the grounds of Buddhist temples in areas along the Thai border, as worshipers celebrate Puja Ketek, or Temple Worship, flocking by the thousands to major temples; important performances are staged in Tumpat and Bachok districts in Kelantan State and in Perlis State. Two good times to hunt out Chinese street opera and puppet plays in large towns are: at Chinese New Year (February), between the first and fifteenth days of the first lunar month, and the period of the full moon of the seventh lunar month (August–September) during the Festival of the Hungry Ghosts. Look for the large, permanent stages built facing major temples or temporary stages built in the street opposite a temple entrance.

TRANSPORTATION. This is one of the most pleasant and comfortable Asian countries to travel in. Services are efficient, modern, not overcrowded. Daily air flights to major cities. Fast, clean, air-conditioned express trains connect Singapore with Kuala Lumpur and Penang, and continue on to Bangkok. Roads are excellent; by rented car is a convenient way to see out-of-the-way places and to enjoy Malaysia's unspoiled and beautiful tropical countryside. The drive from Kuala Lumpur to the east coast and north to shadow-play country in Kelantan is recommended. Taxis can be hailed in the cities or ordered by phone; they are relatively cheap. Kuala Lumpur and Penang city-bus service is good, if you care to take the time to work out the system.

INFORMATION. English is widely spoken and urban performances are advertised in English-language newspapers. Good listings of plays, concerts, and dance recitals in "Weekly Diary" in *Kuala Lumpur This Week*, published by Kuala Lumpur Tourist Association, free in hotels and at Association office in railway station. *Penang for the Visitor*, issued quarterly by Penang Tourist Association (by the clock tower, Leboh Light), tends to ignore theater but does list important festivals. Useful descriptions of traditional Malaysian performing arts in annual *Malaysia Travel Manual*, available through Malaysian Tourist Information offices overseas.

WHAT TO SEE

Wayang Kulit†† shadow-play is clearly related to Indonesian Wayang Kulit; whether it is a transplanted Javanese form, or was introduced from India, or originated in Malaysia, and then later borrowed Javanese and Thai elements is unclear. Like Indonesian Wayang Kulit, it is performed by a single puppeteer seated before a screen; he manipulates the cast of a score of perforated leather figures, speaks dialogue, chants narration, and sings mood songs. Music of drums, bronze gongs and bowls, oboe (*serunai*, also played in Thai and Cambodian theater), and fiddle (*rebab*, also played in the Javanese gamelan ensemble) accompany him. A special stage has evolved for performing; it is six or seven feet off the ground and is closed on sides and back so that the audience can see only the shadows on the screen, while the puppeteer and musicians are hidden from view.

Closed Wayang Kulit stage, Kuantan district, Pahang State, Malaysia.

Different sets of puppets exist to enact several story cycles. *Ramayana* stories (see **India**) are by far the most popular and often performed in Malaysian Wayang Kulit. They are enacted by brightly, even garishly, painted puppets whose pointed crowns, pursed lips, costume design, and snake on which the figures stand strongly point to their being based on Thai models. Puppets for *Mahabharata* stories (see **India**) are simplified versions of Javanese shadow-puppets: Ardjuna, the chief hero of the cycle, for example, is easily recognized from his curled hair style, delicate body shape, long and tapered nose, downcast gaze, and two movable arms (Thai-influenced puppets have only one movable arm). In Malaysia and Java the figure is essentially the same. Puppets for the *Pandji* cycle of plays also seem to be related to Javanese counterparts. Purely Malaysian figures are the clowns, with hinged jaws and humorously grotesque features. Puppets from several cycles are often part of a puppeteer's set.

Wayang Kulit is performed by 200–300 puppeteers, most of whom live in the northern states of Kelantan and Kedah, and to a lesser extent in Trengganu and Perlis. Performances are usually commissioned; they are hard to find but anyone is free to watch. Or, especially in Kelantan, an entrepreneur stakes out an area in an open field, sets up a stage, hires a troupe to perform, and sells tickets for admission. Performance begins around 9:00 P.M. and can last until 2:00 or 3:00 A.M.; a story will continue over several successive nights. Language is a mixture of Malay, Thai, and Arabic. Style of performance is colorful, forceful, active, and relatively simple. Recommended regional performance, Kota Bharu.

Two interesting folk-dance dramas are native to the region along the Thai border: Menora and Ma'yong. *Menora* †† is a Malay version of Lakon Jatri (see **Thailand**). Its audience is mainly Malaysians of Thai descent. Performances traditionally last through three days and nights. Days are given over to preliminaries in which performers, functioning as shamanistic spirit mediums, go into a trance, and through dance communicate with animistic spirits whose beneficent powers are being solicited on behalf of the person sponsoring the play. At night the Menora story, about the abducted bird-princess Menora (Manohra), is enacted in successive episodes. Three actresses play prince, princess, and other major roles; two or more actors take clown roles. Masks can be worn by the men. Plays other than Menora may be performed, but the primacy of this story is clear from the dramatic form's name. You must seek out a performance. Really tough to locate. Most troupes live in Perlis and Kedah. Because it is an art of immigrant Thai-Buddhists, Menora passes almost unnoticed in the mainstream of Malay-Moslem culture.

Ma'yong †† is an all-female dance-drama, purely Malay in origin and development. It seems to have been the creation of female dancers attached

An actress dances the role of Prince Suton in an
exorcistic performance of the Menora folk-play in
Kedah State in northern Malaysia. (Photo courtesy
Ghulam Sarwar.)

to the Malay court of Patani, perhaps as early as the sixteen hundreds.
Ma'yong, and Ma'yong performers, found strong patronage in later centuries at the courts of the sultans of Kelantan and Trengganu. It fell into
decline in this century, during British rule, but the form is currently being
revived and is receiving considerable attention as an important indigenous
Malay dramatic form. Ten or more female dancers perform all major roles,
male and female; two actors play clowns. Women sing and dance; dialogue is
improvised; action takes place in the round, with members of the cast not in
a scene sitting informally along edges of the acting area. Gentle and appealing
circle dances are a highlight of performances. Music is played by rebab, gongs,
drums, and serunai; it has a distinctly mideastern, Arabic sound. Most old
troupes are now disbanded; a regional performance is extremely rare. In
Kuala Lumpur a new troupe of young players has been formed; you might
see them performing as part of National Day celebrations.

Chinese opera temple stage, Penang, Malaysia.

Chinese opera †† troupes are less numerous now than they were in the past, but many are still around. The trick is to be in the right place at the right time (usually at a Chinese Buddhist festival); the troupes do not play in commercial theaters. Some troupes perform in Hokkienese, others in Teochew or Cantonese dialect. Plays and performing style are traditional (see **China**). Indian nondramatic classical dancing, in several styles, can be seen as part of National Day festivities; dancers are amateurs from the local community. Professional dancers from India also are invited to give concert performances from time to time.

Bangsawan † was a popular commercial dramatic form performed in temporary theaters by traveling troupes until a few years ago. Plays were improvised, based on Islamic and mideastern stories, Malay history, and contemporary life. Bangsawan may have grown out of visits of Jatra troupes from Calcutta, at the end of the last century. Scenes were studded with popular songs and dances to satisfy working-class and country audiences. Star performers were idolized. Bangsawan reached its peak in the 1920s, and declined, almost to extinction, under the pressure of movies and television. A regular, commercial performance is rare these days. The government, through the Federal Land Development Scheme, supports one Bangsawan troupe made up of old-time and younger performers that tours to newly opened settlement areas, carrying government themes of unity and pride to the isolated villages.

Modern drama †† has been cultivated by the Western-educated Malay elite since the English introduced their amateur theatricals in the nineteenth century. Until recently modern drama was a mere pastime. Now, the writing of new plays on Malay subjects is encouraged. The staging of these and translations of Western plays has gained a moderately broad following. Still, there are no professional modern-drama groups, and the playwright at best hopes for a few productions. Performances are fairly frequent in Kuala Lumpur (less frequent in Penang); productions will be by amateur and university groups; quality varies widely. A serious hindrance to the full development of modern drama in Malaysia is strong censorship, under which all play scripts must be submitted for police approval, and controversial material of any kind is forbidden.

WHERE TO GO

KUALA LUMPUR. Capital and largest city in Malaysia. Like Washington, D. C. or New Delhi, a government town lacking its own strong cultural traditions. The center of university life (and hence of modern drama) and a good place to see special performances of traditional plays. A national theater is planned for the future; no theater runs continuously; there are small theaters in the British Council building and Universiti Kebansaan (National University). Don't miss the exceptionally fine exhibit of traditional theater which occupies most of the left wing of the National Museum, at the entrance to Lake Gardens. There are well-designed displays of Malay, Thai, Javanese, and Chinese shadow-puppets, a gamelan ensemble, and full-size scenes depicting Menora and Ma'yong in performance. Free; open daily; Friday closed 12:00–2:00 P.M.

Dewan Bandaran (Town Hall)**. Most-used theater in town; located within Kuala Lumpur Municipal Building. Following the British pattern it is run by the city and rents to any group. Intimate (seats 500); pleasant colonial-style auditorium; orchestra level only; comfortable seats, all reserved; air-conditioned; English-language program. Stage is a mere 24 feet wide; moderately well equipped. Most foreign artists perform here; otherwise usually English-language and Malay-language modern drama by amateur groups.

Panggong Anniversary (Anniversary Stage)**. A large outdoor stage set in beautiful Lake Gardens, an expansive park in the city's western suburbs. Normally free to the public; seating on the grass or on folding chairs; sit where you like. Site of night-long National Day variety programs; go early for a close spot on the grass; thousands of people converge from miles around.

Panggong Derama (Modern Drama Stage)**. Operated by the Malaysian Drama Council of the Malaysian Arts Council; primarily for amateur and community theater; modern drama in English and Malay languages. A converted school building; seats 300; an unprepossessing theater; comfortable atmosphere

Panggong Eksperimen (Experimental Stage)***. At the University of Malaysia. The best theater in Kuala Lumpur. Built in late 1960s; very interesting design; modern; air-conditioned; high ceiling; bleacher seats (about 300) on wheels can be moved; flexible stage can be thrust, or proscenium, or arena style. Used by university groups; modern drama in Malay or English; five or six productions a year.

PENANG. An island off the west coast of Malaysia, increasingly popular as an international resort. Georgetown is the chief city. The population is primarily of Chinese descent; consequently this is a good place to find Chinese glove-puppet plays and opera. Among a number of performance locations and occasions are: the **Snake Temple**, ten miles south of Georgetown, during celebrations honoring the god Chor Soo Kong, triennially on the sixth

Temporary Po The Hi puppet stage, Penang, Malaysia.

day of the first, sixth, and eleventh lunar months (January–February, July, December); at **Geok Sam Soo Temple**, five miles north of Georgetown along the coast at Tanjong Bungah, three nights during the full moon of the first lunar month (February); at the same time, **Yap Temple**, corner of Leboh Pitt and Leboh Armenian in Georgetown; one block away at the end of Leboh Pitt, in Cannon Square, on the permanent stage opposite Khoo Kongsi (or Dragon Mountain Hall, Leong Sam Tong Khoo Kongsi), during the full moon of the fourth lunar month (May); at Tanjong Tokong, along the north coast road, at **Ong Yeah Kong Temple** beginning on the eighteenth day of the tenth lunar month (November–December). The Indian festival of Thaipusam is celebrated with impressive parades of penitents in late January (see **Singapore**). Through the month of December performances of folk dances, martial arts, and often Menora, Wayang Kulit, modern drama, and Bangsawan are arranged as part of Pesta Pulau Pinang (Festival of Penang Island).

Dewan Sri Pinang (Penang Cultural Center, also Municipal Hall)***. Dedicated in 1972; a beautiful structure, but unfortunately a concert hall, not a theater; lacks facilities and equipment for proper staging of drama. Location is magnificent, on harbor front facing the Strait of Malacca. Stunningly huge and airy lobby leads to 1,300-seat auditorium; flat orchestra becomes steeply raked at rear; fairly comfortable seats; air-conditioned; restaurant overlooks water. Operated by Penang city; rents to local and visiting dance, music, and theater groups; occasional performances through the year. Inquire at Penang Tourist Association.

Sasaran (Firing Range Theater)**. The experimental theater of Universiti Sains Malaysia used for student productions by the Performing Arts Program of the university. Arena style; small and intimate; air-conditioned; pleasant atmosphere. Converted from a former indoor firing range. Seats about 250. Four or five productions a year in Malay and sometimes English.

REGIONAL PERFORMANCES

BACHOK DISTRICT, KELANTAN STATE. At Batu Tiga is the largest Thai Buddhist temple in Malaysia. Here large-scale, famous Puja Ketek celebrations (October) normally include Menora performances. Also, look for Menora, Wayang Kulit, and Ma'yong troupes performing along the beach front in Bachok during two-week Cultural Festival in May.

JOHORE BAHRU, JOHORE STATE. Traditional dances and plays are staged October 28 in honor of the birthday of the Sultan of Johore. The city is just across the causeway from Singapore; if you happen to be in Singapore on this day, it is an easy 30-minute car trip.

KOTA BHARU, KELANTAN STATE. The heart of Wayang Kulit country. Wayang Kulit, Ma'yong, and other performances are held in the city July 10–12, to celebrate the birthday of the Sultan of Kelantan.

KUANTAN DISTRICT, PAHANG STATE. For forty miles along the coast north of Kuantan city enterprising local officials have set up signs identifying village performing groups that can be commissioned by passing tourists. Just follow the signs; US$15–20 for any number of spectators; one-hour performance. Wayang Kulit along the beach in Cherating village; *Rodat*††, slow-moving Islamic male dance, in Beserah village; and others. June 7–9 games and sports, dancing, singing, and plays at night celebrate Mermaid Festival at Cherating village. Inquire at the State Tourist Center in Kuantan city; they will handle all arrangements for you.

PEKAN, PAHANG STATE. Various dances, sometimes plays, for birthday of the Sultan of Pahang. Pekan is a small town south of Kuantan, far off the beaten track.

TRENGGANU CITY, TRENGGANU STATE. The birthday of the Sultan of Trengganu is June 26. That night and for two successive nights Wayang Kulit, Menora, Chinese opera, and folk dances are performed in various parts of the city.

Books to Read

GENERAL: James R. Brandon, *Theatre in Southeast Asia* (Cambridge, Mass.: Harvard University Press, 1967); P. L. Amin Sweeney, *The Ramayana and the Malay Shadow-Play* (Kuala Lumpur: National University of Malaysia Press, 1972); Richard Winstedt, *The Malays: A Cultural History* (London: Routledge and Kegan Paul, 1961).

PLAYS: Lloyd Fernando, ed., *New Drama One* and *New Drama Two*, (Kuala Lumpur and London: Oxford University Press, 1972).

Philippines

Three centuries of absolute Spanish domination followed by fifty years of American colonization and another five years of Japanese wartime occupation have produced a nation in search of a cultural and artistic identity. To be Filipino is to be both Asian and Western, traditional and modern, vernacular speaking and fluent in English. This multiplicity of the Philippine national experience is reflected on the Philippine stage. Remnants of ancient rituals, dances, and tribal epics are rooted in pre-Spanish animistic religious practices which tie man to his past generations and to the universal spirit world. Moslem groups in southern Mindanao perform their own music and folk dances (distantly related to those of Indonesia). Christian passion-plays and folk-dramas are focal points of village life throughout many islands. Operetta, an outgrowth of Spanish musical plays and once popular in the cities, is being revived. Urban, Westernized, modern dramas, in English and in vernacular languages, speak through amateur performers to an intense audience of university youth.

Some of the most unusual theater experiences are to be found in the provinces, scattered over many islands, not easy to reach from Manila. They are once-a-year performances that will require considerable planning on your part to reach. There is no professional theater group in the Philippines, but there are professional dance companies. A new and massive Cultural Center of the Philippines in Manila provides a home for national and international theater activity and stands as a concrete symbol of the cultural hopes of Filipinos.

THEATERGOING

Folk and religious performances do not follow any set hours, but Christian festival plays tend to be in the daytime and pagan and Moslem performances tend to be at night. (No symbolism implied.) In the cities a play can start anywhere between 6:00 and 8:30 P.M.; 4:00 P.M. matinees Sunday. Tickets are inexpensive; prices are not advertised; phone orders are not accepted.

SEASON. There is no particular theater season in Manila; summer months are quiet for modern drama, but the slack is more than made up for by touring foreign music and dance groups. Most folk performances, village fiestas, and rituals take place during the dry season, March–May, especially during Easter week. Unfortunately it is not only dry, it is also almost unbearably hot then in the Philippines. The wet season is June–October, and a poor time for village plays.

FESTIVALS. An enormous number of fiestas and religious occasions occur each year in the Philippines. They are never merely "entertainment," though they are in fact entertaining. Animism and Christianity mix in festivals of the Bontac and Ifagao tribes who live in the rugged and nearly inaccessible mountains of central Luzon beyond Bagio city. The Bontac engage in a day-long mock war, *Fagfagto,* to celebrate the planting of sweet potatoes in late spring. Men of the tribe divide into two groups and alternately hurl stones at each other, defending themselves with wooden shields. This is a ritual enactment of earlier times when a tribe jealously guarded its precious cultivated land against interlopers. To bring rain the Bontac chant prayers and perform a ritual rain-dance for three days and nights without cease; the ceremony, *Manerwap,* takes place around a blazing fire on a mountain knoll to the beating of drums and gongs. These and other rituals take place in the deep mountains.

Christian festivals occur throughout the year. Each Catholic church celebrates its annual saint's day with a fiesta, many of these occurring between April and June. During Easter week in scores of towns and villages, tableaus of the Passion of Christ are carried through the streets and week-long passion plays are enacted; some are famous and draw thousands of devout spectators. Nativity plays during Christmas are seen in the Visayan islands.

TRANSPORTATION. Travel between cities in the Philippines by air is relatively inexpensive. It is the easiest way to reach the outer islands to see folk and religious performances. All-expense tours are convenient and are advertised in the papers. If you're adventurous you can try taking bus and ferry to most of the outer islands for a fraction of the cost of air travel; it is

slow, however, and uncomfortable. In Manila you can walk to most theaters
from major hotels, provided you do not wilt in the heat and the night streets
do not put you off. Forget the colorful jitney jeep taxis; use the standard
metered taxis at any hotel; they are quite cheap.

INFORMATION. Many Manila performances are listed in "Calender of
Events" in monthly *Manila Guide* (Board of Travel and Tourist Industry,
corner T. M. Kalaw and A. Mabini streets, Manila). Dates and hours of
events in the three theaters of the Cultural Center of the Philippines (CCP)
are listed in their monthly *Calender of Events*, available at the CCP. Newspaper listings are unpredictable. Many of the plays you will find listed are
secondary- and even primary-school productions. Of course, English is
spoken everywhere, making it relatively easy to obtain information.

WHAT TO SEE

Cenaculo† (or ††), are the devout and often bloody enactments by parishioners
of the Passion of Christ. They are probably in part derived from religious
Auto Sacramentales which were so immensely popular in Spain in the sixteenth and seventeenth centuries, and from Mexican versions of Passion
Plays. Each village, or barrio, where the Cenaculo is performed will have its
own version. Normally the play continues through Holy Week, with a suc-
ceeding scene enacted each day: the Last Supper on Holy Thursday; the
Crucifixion, often extraordinarily realistic in portrayal, on the morning of
Good Friday; Christ's funeral procession that evening; and the meeting
(*salubong*) of the resurrected Christ and Mary on Easter Sunday. The Good
Friday enactments are particularly somber and affecting—hundreds of villagers follow Christ as he painfully drags a great wooden cross through the
dusty streets. They help raise Him high in the air during the crucifixion;
penitents march the route with Christ, flagelating themselves (*penitensiya*)
as an act of personal contrition. Cenaculo is pageant, drama, religious ritual.
For many parishioners Cenaculo *is* the death and resurrection of Christ. It
is an honor to perform; a role may be acted by members of one family for
generations. To the' outside observer, the artistic level will not be overly
impressive, but that is not the point of performance. Recommended regional
performances, Marinduque, Malabon, Cainta.

   Comedia†† is a folk play often seen at saint's day fiestas in the countryside
(especially April–June). Also called Moro-moro (from Moor or Moslem)
because the plot invariably calls for a scene in which a Moslem prince is
defeated by a Christian prince. Comedia was first written by Spanish Catholic
priests and friars in the eighteenth century in support of the Christian faith.
Now it is performed in the vernaculars. Comedia is a gloriously romantic

fairy tale of love and honor, a naïvely staged folk spectacle. A brass band blares out a battle tune, a march, or a quadrille; a tournament for the hand of a princess will be carried out in stiffly chivalrous style, as if out of a medieval tapestry; 30–40 of the handsomest young men and prettiest young women of the village parade proudly in slow-step; prompted by the director, holding the locally-written text, the youthful cast forcefully declaims 8- and 12-beat lines of verse in beautifully cadenced phrases. Action moves from church square to stage and back again; there is elaborately built scenery of castles and palaces. Staid and quite old-fashioned now, Comedia is performed less often than in the past. Recommended regional performance, San Dionisio.

Zarzuela †† (or †††) is Philippine operetta; originally modeled on Spanish Zarzuela. In the 1920s, at its peak of popularity, Zarzuela had become purely Filipino in story, language, and music. Nationalistic, anticolonial Zarzuela were popular at the turn of the century; some were banned by American colonial officials. Light, melodic music is composed for each new play. Professional troupes performed in half-a-dozen commercial theaters until World War II. Now several musical and theatrical research societies dedicated to Zarzuela stage several revivals each year in Manila. Quite delightful—unless you absolutely hate musical comedy. (Theater: Cultural Center of the Philippines.)

Philippine folk dance††† is performed by a number of professional and semiprofessional companies based in Manila. Performers are students or recent graduates who bring freshness and youthful vitality to the stage.

A modern dance performance by the Dance Workshop, Cultural Center of the Philippines. (Photo courtesy the Cultural Center of the Philippines.)

Barangay Troupe is known for authenticity of dance style; Bayanihan Dance Troupe and Fiesta Filipina have gained international reputations touring abroad with smoothly choreographed and smartly costumed dramatic ballets based on folk dance; Western and Philippine dance is mingled in the choreography of Dance Theater Philippines. Apart from authenticity, you are assured of a bright, colorful, entertaining performance regardless of group. (Theater: Cultural Center of the Philippines.) Dinner folk-dance shows are given at a number of hotels.

Modern drama†† is nearly a century old in the Philippines. It became a favored art of the educated elite, for it, along with journalism, seemed to be the ideal medium for reaching the people. This hope faded with the advent of movies, and now TV, but the modern Filipino artist's love affair with the theater continues. Volumes of plays, not always of high quality, continue to be written and published by young playwrights. Plays written in English reach an urban, educated audience; plays in Filipino (Tagalog) and other vernaculars reach a broader public. University dramatic groups are important sponsors of playwrights and of productions. Playwrights Nick Joaquin (his classic *Portrait of the Artist as Filipino*), Virginia Moreno, Severino Montano, and A. G. Hufana, and director Rolando Tinio are well known.

The future of modern drama in the Philippines is unclear. In spite of enormous talent and dedication a professional theater has not yet evolved; audiences remain fragmented among different language groups; audiences are not yet of sufficient size. President Marcos, in proclaiming martial law in 1972, abolished freedom of speech. Theater censorship is now in force. Traditional dramatic forms will go on as usual, as will the Manila Theater Guild, which produces the latest London and Broadway fluff in English; whether serious local drama can exist under these sad circumstances remains to be seen.

WHERE TO GO

MANILA. Manila is the complete center of Philippine urban theater. (There is almost no reason to go to other large cities except as way stations while searching for folk or religious drama.) Downtown Manila has six theaters; several others, in schools, are in outlying districts of the city.

Cultural Center of the Philippines (CCP)****. This is the architectural showpiece of the entire Philippines. Completed in 1969 at a cost of US$15 million. It contains several buildings with more planned. On its three stages you can see the choice presentations of the city; three or four offerings a week; one or two performances of each, as a rule. The central structure is an enormous raised cube; spiraling staircases lead into a maze of interconnecting interior lobbies, corridors, snackbars, restaurants, theater library,

Cultural Center of the Philippines, Manila.

lecture rooms, and art exhibition halls. The main space is occupied by the
CCP Theater; seats 2,000 in broad, well-raked orchestra and two balconies;
sinfully soft seats; in spite of its size, sound projects with crystal clarity up to
the last row; I love the towering view from the second balcony (never full,
costs pennies for a seat); air-conditioned; English program. Excellently
equipped and huge stage; too large for most drama; rents primarily to symphony, ballet, Filipino dance, Zarzuela, and Western opera groups. Each
year a dozen or more major American and European groups perform here.
In the rear of the main building is **Munting Dulaan** (CCP Little Theater),
opened in 1972. Seats 402 in steeply raked orchestra; movable ceiling baffles
contribute to superb acoustics; air-conditioned; good stage facilities. Deep
pile carpets underfoot; natural wood and concrete textures; an exceptionally
warm, intimate, pleasant place to see plays; sumptuous without being ornate.
Rents to any small musical or drama group; many below-standard amateur
and school plays; carefully check schedule before going.

A separate **Folk Arts Theater** was inaugurated in 1974. An overpowering
structure, the covered amphitheater can seat 10,000; huge, broad stage;
designed for folkloric pageants and mass music and dance presentations.
Low admission prices; be sure to bring binoculars if you aren't in the front
rows. The CCP is the home of the CCP Philharmonic Orchestra and the
CCP Dance Company; it has no resident theater company, yet. The CCP is
a beautiful complex of buildings, brilliantly designed; it helps fill a glaring
need for good theater facilities in Manila. Yet its sheer, monumental size,
its imposing location, armed guards at the doors during the day are intimidat-

ing; and in this day and age I did not expect to find parterre boxes, where an elite can sit in snobbish privacy.

Open Air Auditorium***. A large, excellently maintained outdoor amphitheater; seats 4,000 on cement benches; high curved wall serves as backdrop and sound baffle (and tends to dwarf performers). In immaculately kept Luneta (Rizal) National Park in the center of Manila. A people-oriented park; at night thousands of couples and families stroll through its gardens, past fountains, restaurants, and Rizal Monument; performances most Saturdays are free; performers are usually only school and amateur groups.

Philamlife Auditorium **. Private hall in office building; built in 1961. Pleasant, warm atmosphere; seats 780 in long, narrow orchestra; comfortable seats; no stage equipment. A popular place in the middle of town for music concerts, dance, and some amateur drama. Rents to any group.

Rajah Sulaiman Theater-in-Ruins **. Unusual outdoor theater built within ruined walls of Fort Santiago. Good example of environmental staging: action takes place on three or four separate platforms, on the crumbling walls, up and down flights of stairs, and in corridors that lead out of sight into the interior of the fort. Audience sits on 300–400 chairs (some swivel) scattered in groups on the ground; audience and stage area bounded by walls open to the sky. Managed by National Parks Commission and used primarily by the Philippine Educational Theater Association (PETA). At night ruins are floodlighted; a bit Hollywoodish, but worth a visit even if there is no production.

REGIONAL PERFORMANCES

CAINTA VILLAGE, RIZAL PROVINCE. Cenaculo during Holy Week is famous. Thursday evening Last Supper and Friday Crucifixion are followed early Easter morning by meeting of Christ and Mary. Can easily be reached by car or bus from Manila.

KALIBO, AKLAN PROVINCE, PANAY ISLAND. Ati-atihan Festival† (Festival of the Aborigines) is celebrated third week of January. Dancers and bands parade through the streets all that week reaching climax over the weekend. Supposedly dedicated to Saint Nino, the festival celebrates the peace which Malay invaders from Borneo forged 750 years ago with Negrito aborigines. Celebrants dress as aborigines, or in wild clown costumes. Not a play; a tropic Mardi Gras. Far from Manila; limited accommodations.

MALABON and *NAVOTA*, neighboring towns in Rizal Province. Cenaculo noted for Good Friday flagellation of masked penitents. Stripped to the waist, young men lacerate their backs with rope whips to which fragments of glass have been glued and prostrate themselves in the street while others whip them. Though forbidden by the church the ritual persists, suggesting deep religious belief of penitents. Can be reached by car or bus from Manila.

MARINDUQUE ISLAND. Site of an unusual Holy Week play, usually called Morion Festival or *Pugutan*††, "beheading." Men from three villages —Boac, Gasan, and Mogpog—combine forces Good Friday through Sunday to enact the story of Roman centurion Longinus. Blind, Longinus' sight is restored by the blood of the crucified Christ striking his eyes; he proclaims the divinity of Christ to the Romans; he is beheaded. Performers wear great masks and are costumed as soldiers. Climax of the pageant play is the chasing of Longinus, his capture, his parade to the execution grounds, and his beheading on Easter Day. This can be a madhouse; Marinduque is just south of Manila; thousands of tourists throng the area. The simple way is to fly in on a tour; it's not expensive; many tours are set up by travel agents in Manila.

SAMAL, BATAAN PROVINCE. Known for the religious fervor of Good

Easter folk performance in the Philippines. Longinus, the centurion whose blindness was cured by the blood of Christ, is beheaded as the climax to the Morion or Pugutan Festival, Marinduque Island. (Photo courtesy the Philippine Tourist and Travel Association.)

Friday crucifixion of Christ during Cenaculo performance. Three-hour ritual enactment takes place in village square. Car or bus; 60 miles from Manila.

SAN DIONISIO, RIZAL PROVINCE.   Comedia presentation before the village church, one month or so after Easter (date is variable). The closest site to Manila for seeing Comedia.

VIGAN, ILOCOS SUR.   This area was one of the earliest to be in contact with Spain. A large procession goes through the city on Holy Monday, making stops at 14 Stations of the Cross. Lamentations to the Virgin Mary are sung in folk style to guitar accompaniment. Two and a half hours from Manila by air.

Books to Read

GENERAL: James R. Brandon, *Theatre in Southeast Asia* (Cambridge, Mass.: Harvard University Press, 1967).

PLAYS: Jean Edades, *Short Plays of the Philippines* (Manila: Benipayo, 1958); Alberto S. Florentine, *Outstanding Filipino Short Plays* (Manila: Filipiniana, 1961).

Singapore

S ingapore is basically a Chinese city, with large Malay, Indian, and Ceylonese minorities. Efficient government services, modern hotels, good and cheap food, help make Singapore a pleasant stopping place. Unlike most tropical cities, it is dynamic and strongly business minded. It is not a major theater city, but foreign music and drama troupes often stop off here and, with a little luck in timing, you could see Chinese opera and puppet-plays.

THEATERGOING

Singapore has several fine theaters. They are rental houses, used one or two nights a week. Audiences are small; a single performance is usual. Curtain time ranges from 6:00 to 8:30 P.M. Tickets are moderately priced; you can conveniently buy tickets downtown at: Cold Storage Supermarket, 176–184 Orchard Road; C. K. Tang, 310 Orchard Road; and Robinson's, 11 Raffles Place. Chinese opera and puppet-plays are normally performed in the street; you can watch free of charge; some spectators bring their own chairs. Malay and Chinese drama used to be performed nightly at Great World, Gay World, and New World amusement parks; following racial disturbances in 1971 performances in the parks were banned. They may be allowed again in future. Inquire of the Tourist Board.

SEASON. Wet and dry seasons are less marked in Singapore than in neighboring countries; plays are staged in all months of the year. February through April is particularly good for outdoor performances.

FESTIVALS. The Indian festival Thaipusam, honoring the god Subraman-
yam, is in late January. Devotees parade in procession carrying decorated
frames attached to their bodies by steel spikes which pierce the flesh; com-
panions, dancing and singing to the sounds of cymbals, horns, and drums
accompany the penitents. Processions begin at Suppiah Temple, Keong Saik
Road, and at Perumal Temple, Serangoon Road, ending at Chettiar Temple,
Tank Road, where devotees walk on glowing coals to prove their faith.
Thaipusam rituals are not for the squeamish. You will almost certainly find
Chinese opera running for several nights around the fifteenth day of the
Chinese New Year (February), and for the Feast of the Hungry Ghosts during
full moon of the seventh lunar month (August–September). For nine nights
of the Kiu Wang Yah festival, beginning on the first day of the ninth lunar
month (October), dragon processions wind through the streets, and puppet-
plays and operas last all night.

TRANSPORTATION. Because Singapore is compact (in spite of its two
million population), you can walk to many theaters. Though hot, it is a
beautiful city for walking. Metered taxis are everywhere in the city; just hail
one; average ride is less than US$1. Many operas that you will find out about
will be in villages, 5–10 miles out of town; even this distance is not expensive
by taxi. The bus service is excellent, if you care to sort out the route system.

INFORMATION. Singapore is a superbly organized city; you can very
easily find out everything there is to see. Read the *Straits Times* for daily
listings. *Singapore Weekly Guide*, free, weekly, distributed by the Singapore
Tourist Promotion Board (Tudor Court, Tanglin Road) tells you everything
that is going on: ballet, music, drama, and—miracle of miracles—Chinese
opera in the streets (with addresses, dates, and hours). Last time there, I found
11 street performances thanks to the *Guide*. English is widely spoken.

WHAT TO SEE

In Singapore when they say "I'm going to see a Wayang" it can mean any
kind of play. Chinese Wayang†† is the Singapore–English way of saying
Chinese opera. Between 10 and 15 troupes perform in various southern styles,
using Hokkien, Teochew, Hainanese, Cantonese, or Hakka, the Chinese
dialects most widely spoken in Singapore. You will not be able to see Ching
Hsi here (only a small fraction of the population is Mandarin speaking). The
performance style and plays are basically traditional; acrobatic scenes are
popular (see **China**). To keep up-to-date, troupes may insert modern songs.
Professional troupes perform both on Singapore island and, when invited by
communities of Chinese in Malaysia, cross the causeway and perform there.
It is rare to run across Chinese opera playing in a regular theater. The usual

performance is in a Buddhist temple compound or in a roped-off area of the street, either in the city of Singapore or in a village a few miles into the country-side. Chinese puppet-plays are given in the same locations and under the same circumstances as Chinese opera. A small but ornate stage is set up in the street or by a temple. There are two types, a string-puppet play, rather uncommon, and the more popular *Pu-tai-hi*† (or ††) glove-puppet play (also performed in Taiwan, Malaysia, and Java). Puppet-plays are intended for children.

You can see Chinese, Indian, and Malay folk dances—such as the Ronggeng courting dance and the Candle Dance—with a minimum of fuss at the government sponsored Instant Asia Cultural Show at **Pasir Panjang Paradise** (195 Pasir Panjang Road), daily at 11:00 A.M. Look for classical Indian dance concerts in December and January, performed by local amateur dancers or by guest artists invited from India (Victoria Theatre). *Aneka Ragam Ra'ayat*, People's Concerts, are sponsored by the Ministry of Culture. Given outdoors in city parks, they include Chinese, Malay, Indian, and Ceylonese music and dances. Their purpose is to encourage among the people of Singapore's various cultural communities an interest in cultures other than their own. Free and open to the public. Call Tourist Board for times and places.

Interest in Western performing arts is perfunctory. There is no professional modern drama. University groups stage plays in Chinese (Cultural Centre Theatre). The foreign community has its Stage Club for English-language amateur productions; soloists and small musical groups from Europe and America perform under the auspices of the Singapore Musical Society; the Singapore Ballet Academy has a season of several weeks (Victoria Theatre).

WHERE TO GO

Cultural Centre Theatre**. Very small house (350 folding chairs); supposedly air-conditioned but wasn't working when I last visited; flat orchestra and tiny balcony; stage opening a mere 25 feet: no stage equipment. A utilitarian concert hall; rents to small amateur music and drama groups. Productions seldom listed in publications. Phone box office for information.

National Theatre ***. Enormous, modern, semiopen amphitheater built up against a beautifully landscaped hillside. Has 3,200 permanent seats; front and middle sections cushioned; other sections wood or metal; on a lovely spot high and in the back, can sit on grass. A cantilevered roof covers all seats, leaving sides and back open. If you have binoculars, bring them. Well-equipped stage 95 feet wide; revolving stage; full flies; elaborate sound system. So large is suitable only for big musical and dance shows. Operated by National Theatre Trust; rents to any group; may be even secondary-school plays here.

Singapore Conference Hall****. Severely modern structure of glass and concrete; built in 1965; seats 1,200; very comfortable seats; air-conditioned. A concert hall; lacks stage equipment. Rents primarily to music groups; large visiting groups play here; productions always listed in publications.

Victoria Theatre***. Singapore's prestige theater. Located in a beautiful area where Singapore River meets the harbor. A colonial era building (also contains **Victoria Memorial Hall**); completely reconstructed in 1959; air-conditioned; seats 1,000 in orchestra and balcony; warm and congenial atmosphere though not luxurious; bars off lobby; well-equipped stage for drama. Rents to any group; the favored theater for drama because of its moderate size and good facilities.

Wisma Theatre**. This is a strange one. Part of the Wisma Indonesia complex of buildings containing Indonesian Embassy, arts and crafts shops, restaurants, and stores built in 1960s by the Sukarno government as a showcase for Indonesian culture. A good little theater; seats 500 on well-raked orchestra; very comfortable seats; air-conditioned; stage moderately well-equipped. The only regularly operating theater the last time I was in Singapore. Bill varies, but usually rents to professional Chinese troupe; two shows a day seven days a week; a modern comedy and a variety show combined; not very good, but unique. Not advertised or listed in publications. Buy your ticket at the door.

Thailand

T hailand has a rich theatrical culture. For more than five centuries the Thai (or Siamese) have shared and exchanged drama, music, and dance forms with neighboring Cambodia, Burma, Laos, China, and Malaysia. The glory of Thai theater is, of course, classical dance-drama. There are two distinct types of shadow-play. Perhaps 100 troupes in the rural areas perform popular operas and folk-dance plays. Chinese opera and marionette plays are staged at fairs. Unfortunately, almost none of this wealth of theater is easy to see. It is a long way into the provinces to find folk and popular plays; few tourists travel in the outlying areas. Classical theater is limited to Bangkok and performances there are few and *very* far between. It is a dilemma that must be resolutely dealt with, if you are going to see Thai theater.

Plan your trip to Bangkok carefully; try to find out in advance whether a classical dance-drama is being staged at that particular time or not. You can go to three different provincial regions and find different dramatic forms. To the north, popular opera and Chinese opera; to the northeast, Lao-style sung-drama; and to the south, shadow-plays and folk-dance plays.

THEATERGOING

Be prepared to hunt for every play you eventually see in Thailand, whether it is in Bangkok or in provincial towns. City performances begin 8:00–8:30 P.M. and often last until midnight. Buy your tickets at the door. Outdoor folk performances in the countryside may last through the night. Popular opera troupes play nightly in miserable commercial theaters, often made of palm thatch and bamboo framework; they can be pretty uncomfortable.

SEASON.   Theater follows the seasons in Thailand. In Bangkok and to the north, November–February is dry, relatively cool, the time for most festival performances; March–June is dreadfully hot, but popular theaters in the provinces run full blast; when the rains come, July–October, theater stops. In the south, December is dry and the time for fair and festival performances; the best time for shadow-plays in the south is the hot season, February through September.

FESTIVALS.   Your best bet in finding a performance in Thailand is to seek out a fair or a festival; invariably there will be one or two troupes set up in the open to draw the crowds. Most provinces sponsor a yearly fair. Fair dates change, but during the first two weeks in December there are likely to be fairs in Lampang, Phitsanulok, Chiengmai, Sukothai, in the north; Udon, Khon Kaen, in the northeast; Bandon, Nakon Srithammarat, Phuket, Trang, Pattalung, Songkhla, in the south. All are large provincial cities. At Bandon's annual fair I've seen popular opera, folk dance-drama, Chinese opera, and shadow-plays on the same night; at the Sukothai fair, I've found popular opera, Chinese opera, folk dances, Thai boxing, movies, and a beauty contest simultaneously vying for an audience. There may even be monkey plays for children. Look for signs of a performance at Buddhist temples. Many temples have an annual festival with theater in the courtyard. Three Buddhist holidays celebrated nationally can be occasions for theater: Magha Puja, the anniversary of the gathering of Buddha's disciples, the night of the full moon of the third lunar month (April); Ok Pansa, celebrating the end of Buddhist Lent (usually in October); and Lov Krathong, Festival of Lights, during the full moon of the eleventh lunar month (December-January).

TRANSPORTATION.   Domestic air flights reach major provincial cities. A fast, comfortable express train connects Bangkok with cities in the south. Open-sided buses cover the sparsely populated north and northeast; for the hardy; slow, cheap, and fun. Bangkok is a car driver's nightmare; dense traffic; a pall of diesel fumes in the air; dripping hot; maddeningly slow, it can take an hour to get through the central district. Plan your city trips accordingly, for you won't want to blithely cross the city several times a day. Taxis at hotels are hire cars; drivers speak English; quite expensive. Much cheaper are cruising taxis, drivers do not speak English; have the name of your destination written in Thai script; set price before you leave (the meter in the taxi is never used). You can walk in the Pra Mane Ground area, between Silpakorn Theater, Lok Muong Temple, and the National Museum; otherwise, distances are too great and the heat too oppressive to walk to theaters in Bangkok.

INFORMATION. You will not find much useful published information to help in your theatergoing. Classical dance performances may be mentioned in English newspapers (the *World*, the *Nation*, and the *Bangkok Post*). Tourist Organization of Thailand (corner Raj Damnoen and Dinsaw roads) can tell you dates and locations of religious festivals; they keep pretty accurate and up-to-date information on provincial festivals as well. Popular theaters are never advertised or listed; you have to go to the theater and see for yourself if anything is playing. Since the chances are you will be in Bangkok when no classical dance-drama is playing, you might consider seeing classical dance at a restaurant. Half-a-dozen dinner shows to choose from; usually good dancing by well-trained, handsome, professional performers; Thai dinner; elegant atmosphere; about US$6–9.

WHAT TO SEE

Thai classical dancing goes back to the fourteenth century, possibly earlier. In 1342 Thai armies captured the Cambodian capital of Angkor and brought back, as prisoners, the Khmer king's court dancers and musicians. To this day, Thai and Cambodian classical dance-dramas are similar in dance style; the Thai *pi phat* musical ensemble of bamboo xylophones, bronze bowls, oboe, bell cymbal, and drums is the same as the Cambodian *pin peat* ensemble; costuming is similar as well. Two main classical-drama forms are a product of this tradition.

Lakon Nai†††† is quintessential female court dance-drama. Massed dance choruses of beautiful, exquisitely costumed young women play both male and female parts; they move in delicate unison patterns, dipping, rising, arms flowing from gesture to gesture, faces fixed in a subtly alluring half-smile. Star actresses play Prince Inao (from the Javanese *Pandji* story) and the several princesses he loves; *Inao* plays are the major items in the Lakon Nai repertory. Performers are not masked and they speak their own dialogue; there is no narrator; a seated female chorus sings verses that are danced. In the days of Thai monarchy, dancers were members of the royal harem and only guests of the royal patron were allowed to witness a performance. The dramatic form in Cambodia parallel to Lakon Nai is Lakon Kbach Boran.

Khon†††† is male masked dance-drama. Stately processions of warriors, demons, and monkeys set a stirring, masculine tone; long battles culminate in acrobatic group poses; two narrators recite sections of narration and dialogue, as the actors mime the meaning of the words. Actors never speak, for in old-style Khon the all-male cast wore masks, with towering crowns, which covered the entire head. Nowadays, under the influence of Lakon Nai, actresses play the roles of women and of refined men; chosen for their beauty, they are not, of course, masked. Selected episodes from the Thai version of the

Classical court dancers performing in Lakon Nai style before outdoor pavilion in the grounds of the National Museum, Bangkok. (Photo courtesy Thai Public Relations Department.)

Ramayana (see **India**) make up the repertory; no other stories are done in Khon. Khon is the Thai equivalent of Cambodian Lakon Khol.

Today, full-length Lakon Nai and Khon plays are performed only by the Silpakorn Troupe of the Department of Fine Arts, in Bangkok. Consisting of some 300 performers, musicians, teachers, and directors, it is the direct descendant of court-supported royal ballets that were ended in the 1930s. The troupe takes other play repertories as well and performs them in classical dance style: *Lakon Nok*†††, previously a popular, professional dramatic form, in which local legends and Buddhist *Jataka* stories such as the famous *Prince of the Golden Sea Shell* are dramatized; *Lakon Jatri*†† (or †††), a folk-dance drama based on the *Manohra* story that was introduced to Bangkok from the southern provinces; and others as well. (Theaters: Silpakorn and Sangkhit Sala.)

A third important court drama was *Nang Yai*†††† shadow-play. Huge leather puppets, with entire scenes incised in them, and smaller, life-sized puppets of Rama, Sita, and Hanuman enact episodes from the *Ramayana*. Two narrators recite the epic tale; a dozen puppeteers carry the puppets, moving before and behind a huge screen, lighted from behind by a blazing fire; the puppeteers must be dancers, too, for they impart life to the puppets,

Khon performance at the Sangkhit Sala in Bangkok. Actress playing Rama balances on the back of the white monkey Hanuman. (Photo courtesy Thai Public Relations Department.)

held high overhead, with dancing motions of their own lithe bodies. A troupe would perform on state occasions, for funerals, and for other important events. Nang Yai is almost a vanished art today; there is no troupe in Bangkok capable of performing; two temple troupes, composed of villagers, are known to exist and apparently that is all. It is a magnificent and dying art. Should a rare performance be arranged in Bangkok, don't miss it. Cambodian Nang Sbek and Thai Nang Yai are almost identical.

Small shadow-puppets, *Nang Talung*† (or ††), enact many kinds of stories using a technique more closely related to Indonesian and Malaysian Wayang Kulit than to Nang Yai. A single puppeteer sits before the screen, manipulates a puppet in each hand, narrates the story, and speaks each character's dialogue. Puppets are translucent and carved in the distinctive style of costumed Lakon Nai and Khon dancers. The home of Nang Talung is southern Thailand. Perhaps as many as fifty Nang Talung puppeteers perform in the southern provinces, moving from fair to fair and from festival to festival during the dry season. As an art form, it is a crude hodgepodge of popular, folk, and classical elements; a minor art, it is interesting to see primarily as one example of the many types of shadow-play in Asia. Recommended regional performances at fairs in Trang, Songkhla, Bandon; competition of troupes at Nakon Srithammarat during Lov Krathong, Festival of Lights.

Lakon Jatri††, in its folk form, is an extremely interesting southern Thai dance-drama. Performers, originally only men, specialized in shamanistic spirit-possession dances and in enacting the Buddhist *Jataka* play, *Manohra*. Manohra is the name of the mythical *kinnari* maiden—half bird, half human —who marries the human prince, Suton, is burned, rises to heaven, and in the end is reunited with her husband. The play can be performed in a dozen or more episodes, over as many nights. Lakon Jatri is popularly called Manohra, or just 'Nora. The long solo dances can be remarkably refined; dance style seems to have been influenced by Indian classical dance; performers must be quite versatile, for they sing, act, mime, and speak dialogue, as well as dance. Traditionally three performers take all roles; today women as well as men are in troupes; plays other than *Manohra* may be performed. Many troupes tour the southern provinces during the dry season; you will be sure to find Lakon Jatri at every southern fair.

Likay† (or ††) is popular Thai opera. Troupes, perhaps as many as one hundred, travel the length of Thailand, performing at fairs, at temple festivals, and in rickety, filthy commercial theaters in the cities and towns. Likay is third-rate, popular theater at its saddest. It began in the early part of this century, when popular performers staged court plays, after having been taught the rudiments of classical dance and music; in the 1920s it was all the rage; today, Likay performers are, almost without exception, untrained and untalented. Classical pi phat music is played and performers make tentative dance gestures entering and exiting, and that is about all that is left of the classical influence. Actors improvise song lyrics. Even the play will be improvised in the course of performing, and may be stretched over as many nights as the audience wishes. Play sources are legends, history, and local stories. Until recently you could see Likay almost every night of the year in Bangkok in one of two decrepit and foul-smelling theaters—Bang Krabue, in Bang Krabue market, or Hom Hwan, in Bamglampoo market—in the area just north of the Silpakorn. But lately both theaters have fallen on bad times; they are dark through most of the year. To see Likay now, you have to find a festival performance (in Bangkok or at a provincial fair) or go to one of the commercial theaters that can be found in most provincial cities.

Likay plays are put to Lao reed-organ music in *Mohlam Luong*† in northeast Thailand where the population is culturally Lao and Lao-speaking (see **Laos**). There are 15–20 *Chinese Opera*†† troupes that perform for festivals and at fairs in Thailand. A *Marionette*†† troupe doing *Ramayana* stories, can sometimes be seen performing in the open in Bangkok; its home is Thon Buri, just across the river.

University and amateur groups stage *Modern Drama*†† in Bangkok; translations of Western plays and modern scripts. Modern drama is not a significant aspect of Thai theatrical life as yet; audiences are small and restricted to a Western-oriented elite. (Theater: Bangkok, Culture Hall.)

WHERE TO GO

BANGKOK. The only significant theater buildings are in Bangkok. You can expect to see outdoor performances of Chinese opera, Likay, and perhaps marionette plays many times during the year at temples; at Vaijiravudh Fair, honoring King Rama VII, from around November 25 until December 5, at the fairground behind the Royal Palace; and on the King's birthday, December 10, and for several days after, at Lumpini Park (corner Rama IV and Raj Damri roads) or at Pra Mane Ground (between the Royal Palace and the National Museum). A collection of Nang Yai shadow-puppets and several pi phat ensembles are exhibited in the National Museum, a superb museum you should not miss. Likay, Lakon Nai, and Khon can be seen on TV from time to time.

Culture Hall***. A modern auditorium; air-conditioned; seats 900 comfortably in push-back seats. Large stage; lacks stage equipment. Rents to any group; you are as likely to find a secondary-school class play as a fine classical-dance concert; perhaps one or two performances a week; elite audience.

Lok Muang (City Pillar)**. On the spot where, in 1782, King Rama I founded the city of Bangkok, a small walled edifice stands in commemoration of the event and houses the stone pillar itself. Also, this is the one place in Bangkok where you can always see a traditional play; not a very good performance (in fact, pretty bad), but it's there. As an offering of thanksgiving for having received a blessing, a person will hire 10 minutes, an hour, a day, even three or four days of performance, and dedicate it to the gods. Grateful believers reserve time months in advance. From around nine each morning until midafternoon, all-female troupes do third-rate Lakon Nok and Lakon Jatri; pi phat music; performers sing, dance, and speak dialogue; stage is 10-by-15-foot section of tiled floor along left side of temple building; a bench is in the center; at the back are two curtained doors for entering and exiting; an old woman prompts from the side, a book in her lap. An offertory performance is not actually intended for a human audience (similar performances go on in back alleys where they are never "seen"), but old women and children often sit and watch all day; casual visitors to the temple pause for a few minutes at the back, then pass on. It's bad art but fascinating.

Sangkhit Sala (Music and Dance Stage)**. A simple raised platform set at the edge of the National Museum lawn; has a permanent backing; ramps lead to the stage from either side; musicians sit to audience left. You sit on the grass wherever you want; it is always crowded; come a little early for a good viewing spot. From mid-November through May, most Sunday afternoons, classical dances and episodes from Khon, Lakon Nai, Lakon Nok, or Lakon Jatri plays. As changes occur often, check newspapers and Tourist Organization. Performed by graduates of the Department of Fine Arts (not members of the Department's famous Silpakorn troupe, however). Actors are handsome; female dancers extremely appealing; costuming superb; dancing is of a high standard; direction unimaginative. The scale of performance is necessarily less impressive than when the Silpakorn Troupe performs in the large Silpakorn Theater next door. By all means see this if you are in Bangkok on a Sunday; the atmosphere is very pleasant; the performance first rate. It's your best chance of seeing something of classical theater. Popular music (sometimes rock) concerts Saturday afternoon.

Silpakorn (National Theater)****. A capacious, beautiful theater designed for classical dance drama; opened in 1965. The outside is boxily im-

Sangkhit Sala, Bangkok, Thailand.

pressive perhaps; it is the interior that is truly eye-catching. Behind a broad, 55-foot stage opening is a well-equipped stage area; there is a huge dance forestage, 70 feet wide and 30 feet deep, gently raked for good viewing; main and forestage connect through a proscenium door on each side; flanking the dance stage are raised platforms where musicians and singing chorus sit in view of the audience. Seats 1,400 in broad, shallow orchestra and balcony; wide, soft seats; air-conditioned; spacious lobbies; English section in program. This is the perfect theater for Thai classical dance drama. In fact it is too good, it is so expensive to maintain that it cannot be used often. Foreign troupes, movies, conventions, political rallies, musical shows, and the like rent it occasionally. Ironically, the Department of Fine Arts staged 100 performances a year in their old shed theater before it burned down; now in their marvelous new one they stage far fewer. Between November and April, two to four classical plays are usually staged, each playing four weekends as a rule. Occasionally amateur troupes stage classical plays as well. If you manage to catch a Khon, Lakon Nai, Lakon Nok, or Lakon Jatri performance by the Silpakorn Troupe in this theater you are in for a memorable treat; the productions are meticulously executed and always on a grand scale. Good luck.

Silpakorn, Bangkok, Thailand.

Books to Read

GENERAL: James R. Brandon, *Theatre in Southeast Asia* (Cambridge, Mass.: Harvard University Press, 1967); Thai Culture New Series pamphlets *Khon Masks*, *The Khon*, and *Shadow Play* (Bangkok: Fine Arts Department, 1962–1969); Dhanit Yupho, *The Khon and Lakon* (Bangkok: Fine Arts Department, 1963).

PLAYS: Fern Ingersoll, *Sang Thong* (Rutland, Vt.: Charles E. Tuttle, 1973).

Vietnam

Local and borrowed Chinese artistic impulses have combined to make Vietnamese culture unique. Of all the tropical countries of Southeast Asia, only here has Chinese rather than Indian cultural influence predominated. Theater is ancient in Vietnam. Opera and operetta are major drama forms, performed by professional troupes in most parts of the country—north, central, and south. The backbone of drama in Vietnam is song. If you like the music you will like the drama, whether classical or popular or folk. Most drama is traditional; in the long aftermath of World War II new dramatic forms have been slow to develop.

There have been three traditional centers of theater in Vietnam: Hanoi in the north, Hue in the central provinces, and Saigon in the south. Each city has boasted several important theater buildings, usually open nightly, and every provincial city has had one or more permanent theaters. It has been common practice for troupes to travel from one city to the other.

The state of theater in North Vietnam is not clearly known. The war in the south has, for decades, disrupted theater activities there. Theaters have been destroyed in many provincial cities. In April 1975 a new Revolutionary Government of South Vietnam assumed control; its attitude toward theater and its policies for maintaining and operating theater troupes are, as yet, unknown. Theater conditions described here are certain to change.

THEATERGOING

Theaters try to run nightly whenever possible, usually 8:00 to 11:30 P.M. Tickets are not expensive. Buying at the box office the night of performance or in advance are both common practices. Theater buildings in Saigon are moderately good, usually air-conditioned; they are fair in provincial cities and towns. In most Southeast Asian countries a troupe will perform a different play each night, having as many as a hundred plays in its repertory. Classical opera in Vietnam follows this tradition; popular operetta troupes in the south, however, may run a single play for a month or more.

SEASON. October through December is the best theater season; the weather is slightly cool and dry in the south and pleasantly cool in the north. During the hot season, January–March, all types of drama are performed in numerous locations, but going into hot or stuffy theaters cannot be said to be comfortable. April–September is the season of tropical downpours, which discourage all but a few urban troupes in the better theaters.

TRANSPORTATION. Distances between hotels and theaters are too great for comfortable walking in Saigon. Taxis are plentiful and not expensive; they can be hailed in the street or ordered from the hotel.

INFORMATION. You probably will find little helpful published information in English. The best bet is to ask the hotel manager which theaters are running and how to obtain a ticket. Ask about the theaters listed at the end of this book—their names may have changed but they will be known to local residents. If plays are being performed, it is likely that these theaters are the ones being used. More than in most countries, you will want to ask about theater conditions after you arrive.

WHAT TO SEE

Hat Boi†† (or †††) is Vietnamese classical opera. As early as 1285 Vietnamese were learning Chinese opera through their continued contact with the Chinese. In time, new Vietnamese plays were written; original melodies were composed; and costuming and makeup were altered to suit Vietnamese tastes. However, when you see Hat Boi, you will undoubtedly be struck by how similar it is to Chinese opera—visually, structurally, and in terms of movement patterns and acting conventions. Actors and actresses sing (solos only) to whining fiddles and crashing cymbals; movements are symbolic; brilliant-colored patterns of makeup identify character type; costumes are colorful and formal in cut. In traditional performances there is no scenery; a table and two chairs serve symbolically for any locale. Down through the time of Emperor Tu Duc (1847–1883) emperors supported Hat Boi at their courts; Hue, in central Vietnam, was the royal capital. Court support no longer exists, but the finest Hat Boi troupes are still found in the central provinces of Binh Dinh, Quang Ngai, and Tuy Hoa.

Classical Hat Boi performed at a public theater in Saigon. (Photo courtesy the Embassy of Vietnam, Washington, D.C.)

The appeal of Hat Boi in the twentieth century has declined greatly; it is considered a difficult, esoteric art. No one knows how many troupes play Hat Boi today. You are likely to find the best professional troupes playing in commercial theaters in Da Nang and Qui Nhon; small traveling troupes walk from village to village carrying their costumes and equipment, but it's rather unlikely you will stumble across such a troupe. In Saigon the third-rate troupes that used to play in dingy temple halls and dirty little commercial theaters a few years ago seem to have disappeared. The easiest way to see Hat Boi is on television, usually one night a week. Also, watch for special performances (sponsored by the Conservatory of Drama or private art groups) that will run a single night; will be advertised in English-language papers. These are usually excellent.

Cai Luong†† (or †††) is a kind of light opera or operetta. Since the 1920s it has replaced Hat Boi as the most popular dramatic form with Vietnamese audiences. Its star singers are idolized; their pictures appear in the papers; they earn huge incomes; their songs are played on the radio unceasingly. Cai Luong musical style comes from southern Vietnamese folk songs. The style is suited to love laments and pathetic songs. Audiences dab at tears when a singer launches into the ravishingly beautiful "Vong Co," a love song written 50 years ago that is sung in every play without exception; you will hear "Vong Co," in different guises, 10–15 times in a performance. This and other well-liked melodies are used in all plays; new lyrics are written for each play, however. Cai Luong plays are adapted from Hat Boi (which in turn may have been adapted from a Chinese opera); they are based on Vietnamese history or legend; they are about contemporary life in Saigon. If you have a choice, see a history play for its action and color. Cai Luong is sung and acted in a highly emotional manner; at times the lovely melodic lines and the unabashed emotionalism remind me of Puccini. Cai Luong troupes are particularly susceptible to changes in the political and economic conditions in Vietnam; their audience is drawn from the lower-middle and working classes. It is difficult to know how many professional troupes are active at any given moment, 15–20 perhaps. Go to the provinces and you are likely to find a professional troupe playing in Hue, Da Nang, Nha Trang, My Tho, Can Tho, or Bien Hoa. In Saigon, moderately good Cai Luong is telecast each week, usually on Saturday night. (Theaters: Saigon: Olympic and Quoc Thanh.)

Modern drama, or *Thoai Kich*††, is a new and struggling art form. The average spectator is used to the music and song and action of traditional drama and finds it dull business to watch people sit around a living room and talk, and talk, and talk. One major troupe, Tu Do, is semiprofessional. Amateur and university groups perform in high schools. Adaptations of Western plays and, increasingly, modern Vietnamese plays are staged. Do not expect serious themes; all plays must be approved by an all-powerful government censor. Audiences are small and of the educated elite.

WHERE TO GO

SAIGON. Saigon was "the Paris of the Orient," but the war and the internal combustion engine have denuded the city of much of its former charm. Plays were staged at two commercial theaters regularly; others may have live drama from time to time. (**Hung Dao** and **Nguyen Van Hao** theaters have housed Cai Luong in the past, and might again sometime.)

Olympic Theater**. An older building; quite dingy; seats 1,200 in orchestra and two small balconies; overhead fans; often hot and stuffy; when SRO, chairs are put in the aisle. Stage 35 feet wide; fair stage equipment; hanging microphones float across stage to follow performers. A regular Cai Luong theater; a troupe will run one play for several weeks or a month, then change.

Quoc Thanh***. Theater was shelled and is now renovated; clean and bright; seats 1,500; comfortable, wide seats; air-conditioned. Stage is 45 feet wide; moderately well-equipped. Cai Luong plays here regularly; length of troupe run varies, but usually several weeks.

Book to Read

James R. Brandon, *Theatre in Southeast Asia* (Cambridge, Mass.: Harvard University Press, 1967).

Theater List

CAMBODIA

moha vithei = boulevard

PHNOM PENH

Grand Palace, Moha Vithei Samdach Suthrot. No performances, but rehearsals, when held, may be open to the public; weekdays, 8:00–11:30 A.M. Take taxi.

Krom Silpea Khmer Selai, near Stadium at Phsar Depot (station market). Hours and prices variable. Take taxi.

Phsar Silep, in Silep Market. Hours and prices variable. Take taxi.

Rastea Chantrey, in Tuol Tapuong district. Hours and prices variable. Take taxi.

Theatre Municipal, off Moha Vithei Samdach. Hours and prices variable. Take taxi or cyclo. Coming from the center of town on Moha Vithei 9 Soka, at Victory Monument turn left on Avenue 18 Mars 1970 (formerly Sihanouk Ave.) and go to end; at river, walk right one block; theater is red-and-white-peaked modern building.

CHINA (TAIWAN)

TAIPEI

Kuo Chung Wen Yi Ho-tung Chung Shin, 69 Chunghua Road. Usually 7:30 P.M. Tickets NT$40, 30, 20, 10. Taxi NT$20–25. Or, standing on pedestrian overpass (corner Chunghua and Chengtu roads) with fountains on your right, theater is straight ahead one and a half blocks, on left side of the street, the large square building with military murals on facade.

Kuo Fu Chi-nien Kuan, corner Nanking East and Tunghua South roads. Hours and prices variable. Tickets, often for charity, may be expensive. Take taxi, NT$30–40.

Kuo Li Yi-shu Kuan, Nanhai Road between Chungching So. and Hoping West roads. Next to National Historical Museum in Botanical Gardens. Hours and prices variable. Taxi NT$20–25. Theater is on your left as you enter main park gate on Nanhai Road.

Oscar Music Hall, corner Chunghua and Hengyang roads, in Shin Sheng Theatre Building. Hours and prices variable; see board in front of theater. Taxi NT$15–20. Or, standing on the overpass at Chunghua and Chengtsu roads with railroad tracks at your back, you can see theater at far end of overpass.

World of Today Recreation Center, 52 Omei Street. Phone 36–9751; English spoken. Special tourist matinee: Monday–Friday, 4:30 P.M.; Saturday and Sunday, 5:30 P.M. Tickets NT$50. Regular performance: nightly 7:30 P.M. plus Saturday and Sunday 2:00 P.M. matinee. Tickets NT$40, 32, 20. Sixth floor theater: daily 2:40, 7:00, and 9:20 P.M.; tickets NT$50, 40; buy tickets on third floor. Taxi NT$15–20. Or, standing at fountain on corner of Chunghua and Chentu roads with your back to railroad tracks, go one block down diagonal road on your right, turn left, go two blocks, building is on your left. Go in first entrance for elevators. Sign at entrance reads, in English, "Today's Co."

HONG KONG

City Hall, Edinburgh Place, Hong Kong Island. Phone H-229928, H-229511, H-227271; English spoken. Usually 8:00 P.M. Prices variable. From Kowloon, take Star Ferry to Hong Kong Island Terminal, the theater is 150 feet to your left as you exit.

Lai Chi Kok Amusement Park, in Lai Chi Kok, about 6 miles northwest of downtown Kowloon. Theaters in park open 8:00 to 11:00 P.M. Park admission HK$1. Theater admission HK$3, 2, 1. On the edge of the city and easy to get to: take bus No. 6 (not 6a or 6c) from Star Ferry, or along Nathan Road, to end of line at park entrance or take taxi for HK$6–8.

INDIA

marg = road
saranee = lane

NEW DELHI

All India Fine Arts and Crafts Society Hall, corner Rafi Marg and Red Cross Road. Usually 6:30 P.M. Tickets Rs10, 5, 3. Taxi Rs2–5.

Ferozeshah Kotla Grounds, opposite Delhi Gate, corner Lal Nehru Marg and Bahadur Shah Zafar Marg. Phone 27–4857, 27–2039; English spoken. Hours and prices variable. Taxi Rs2–5.

Kamani Auditorium, Lytton Road between Canning and Ferozeshah roads. Phone 38–6428; English spoken. Usually 6:30 P.M. Prices vary. Next to Rabindra Bhavan. Taxi Rs2–5.

National School of Drama Outdoor Theater, in garden behind Rabindra Bhavan (see below). From main entrance go left 100 feet across lawn and through garden.

Rabindra Bhavan, corner Ferozeshah and Lytton roads. Phone 38–7246; English spoken. A 15-minute walk from Connaught Place: take Barakhamba Road to the traffic circle. Taxi Rs1–3.

Sapru House, Barakhamba Road, corner of Ferozeshah Road. Hours and prices vary. Across the traffic circle from Rabindra Bhavan. Taxi Rs1–3.

Triveni Garden Theater, in Triveni Kala Sangham building, 205 Tansen Marg. Phone 44–297; English spoken. Across the street from Sapru House and across the traffic circle from Rabindra Bhavan. Taxi Rs1–3.

BOMBAY

Bhang Wedi, Bhang Wedi crossing, Kalbadevi Road. Tickets Rs4, 3, 2, 1. Not easy to find: walk north on Kalbadevi Road from Dhobi Talao Circle, pass intersection of South Gandhi Road (formerly Princess St.) about 75 feet, enter long courtyard to your left, theater is at far end. Taxi Rs2–4.

Bharatiya Vidya Bhavan, Pandita Ramabai Road. Phone 35–1461; English spoken. Hours and prices variable. Taxi Rs3–5. Or, take BEST Bus No. 123 north along Netaji Subhash Road (formerly Marine Drive) to Chowpatty Beach, walk one block right up Pandita Rambai Road; theater is imposing sandstone building on corner on your right.

Bhulabhai Desai Auditorium, 178 Backbay Reclamation, off Netaji Subhash Road (formerly Marine Drive). Phone 29–4044; English spoken. Hours and prices variable. Taxi Rs2–4. Or, at International Hotel, face harbor, walk left to first side street, turn left, go 100 feet, auditorium is in red stone Nanji Kalidas Mehta International House on left side of street.

Birla Matushri Sabhagar, 19 New Marine Lines. Phone 29–6707; English spoken. Hours and ticket prices variable. In red building marked "Bombay Hospital Annex." About 200 yards north of Patkar Hall on opposite side of street. Taxi Rs1–3.

Jai Hind Auditorium, A Road, off Netaji Subhash Road (formerly Marine Drive). Hours and prices variable. In Jai Hind College grounds. Taxi Rs1–3. Or, from Hotel Nataraj, face harbor, walk left to first side street, turn left; auditorium is grey building third from corner on your left.

National Centre for the Performing Arts, 89 Bhulabhai Desai (formerly Warden) Road. Phone 36–1777; English spoken. Hours variable. Often free. Take taxi, Rs3–5. On second floor of new, tall office building set back 100 feet from road and facing harbor.

New Hanuman Theater, Industrial Estates, opposite Lalbaug Market. Phone 44–1150; English spoken. Nightly 6:30 P.M. Tickets Rs5, 4, 3, 2. Taxi Rs4–6. Not easy to find. Going north on Babasaheb Ambedkar Road, turn right on S. S. Rao Road, go 100 feet to Lalbaug Market; on right side is thin cement arch marked "Industrial Estates." Enter and turn left after 50 feet.

Patkar Hall, corner Nathibai Thakersey Road and New Marine Lines. Phone 29–4031; English spoken. Hours and prices variable. On Sir Vithaldas Thackersey College grounds, enter gate 4 or 5. About 250 yards north of U.S. Information Service (USIS) on opposite side of street. Taxi Rs1–3.

Rang Bhavan, off Mahapalika Marg at Khobi Talao Circle, in Elphinstone Technical High School compound. Phone 26–4460; English spoken. Taxi Rs2–4. Or, from Dhobi Talao Circle walk south 100 yards on Mahapalika Marg, turn left at first side street; theater entrance is squat pink and cream structure on your left 100 yards in.

Ravindra Natya Mandir, Bavani Road, just off Vir Savarkar Marg. Phone 24–1265; English spoken. Hours and prices variable. Quite far out; take taxi, Rs8–10.

Shanmukhananda Hall, 292 Flank Road. Phone 27–4617, 27–1588; English spoken. Hours and prices variable. A 30-minute taxi ride from downtown, Rs12–16. Or take Central Railroad to King's Circle station, and walk back three blocks.

Shivaji Natya Mandir, N. C. Kelkar Road, near Dadar Station on Western Railroad. Hours and prices variable. Taxi Rs12–14. Or take train to Dadar Station, follow Tilak Road to your left to Plaza Cinema, cross the street and go right 100 yards, go in entry marked "Shivaji Mandir."

Tejpal Auditorium, Forjet Street, two blocks off Peddar Road on Cumballa Hill. Hours and prices variable. Take taxi, Rs4–6.

CALCUTTA

Academy of Fine Arts, Cathedral Road. Opposite Victoria Memorial. Hours and prices variable. A 20-minute walk from downtown: go south on Jawahar Lal Nehru (formerly Chowringhee) Road, turn right into Cathedral Road; on your left about a quarter-mile ahead. Taxi Rs1–3.

Biswaroopa, 2-A, Raj Rajkissen Street. Phone 55–3262. Hours: 6:00 P.M. Thursday; 2:30 and 6:00 P.M. Saturday and Sunday. Tickets Rs10, 7, 5, 2. Hard to find. Set back from crowded street. Taxi driver will know; Rs4–8. If walking, see **Rangana**.

Kala Mandir, fittingly on Shakespere Saranee. Near Acharya Jagadish Chandra Bose Road crossing. Phone 44–9086; English spoken. Hours and prices variable. A 15-minute walk from Park or Grand Hotel: either go left on Park Street to Acharya Jagadish Chandra Bose Road, go right to Shakespere Saranee (next large street) and turn right 100 yards, theater is on your left; or, go south on Jawahar Lal Nehru (formerly Chowringhee) Road, turn left on Shakespere Saranee six blocks, the theater is on your right. Taxi Rs1–2.

Minerva Theater, 7 Beadon Street. Hours: 6:30 P.M. Thursday; 2:30 and 6:30 P.M. Saturday and Sunday. Tickets Rs5, 4, 3. Recommend taxi, Rs5–7. If venturesome, take streetcar north on Jawahar Lal Nehru (formerly Chowringhee) Road for 30 minutes past dozens of musical instrument shops, to Beadon Street, walk right on Beadon 150 yards.

Mukta Angan, at Kalighat Crossing, where Shyma Prasad Mukherjee Road (a continuation of Jawahar Lal Nehru Road) crosses Rash Behari Ave. Phone 46–5277; English spoken. Usually nightly 7:00 P.M. Tickets, Rs3, 2, 1. Difficult to find. Recommend taxi, Rs4–6. Or, take streetcar No. 29 from Maidan (esplanade) south to Kalighat crossing, walk in the same direction past crossing 100 feet; small unmarked entryway on left side of boulevard opens into theater entry corridor.

Rabindra Sadan, corner Acharya Jagadish Chandra Bose and Cathedral roads, near Victoria Memorial. Hours and prices variable. Taxi Rs1–3. Walking, go past the Academy of Fine Arts another 200 yards.

Rangana, Raj Rajkissen Street, off Bidhan Saranee. Phone 55–6846; English spoken. Hours: 6:00 P.M. Thursday; 2:30 and 6:00 P.M. Saturday and Sunday. Tickets Rs10, 6, 3, 1. Difficult to find. Take taxi, Rs3–5. Or, facing Star Theater on Bidhan Saranee walk to your right 50 feet, turn left into narrow Raj Rajkissen Street, pass Biswaroopa Theater (on your right), and about 500 yards ahead (past cattle pens) theater is on your right.

Rung Mahal, Bidhan Saranee. Phone 55–1619; English spoken. Hours: 6:00 P.M. Thursday and Saturday; 2:30 and 6:00 P.M. Sunday. Tickets Rs7, 5, 4, 3. Taxi Rs3–5. Or, facing Star Theater walk right, go 30 feet past Raj Rajkissen Street; theater is through small archway set back from street.

Star, 79 Bidhan Saranee. Phone 55–1139; English spoken. Hours: 6:00 P.M. Thursday and Saturday; 2:30 and 6:00 P.M. Sunday. Tickets Rs10, 7, 5, 2. Recommend taxi, Rs3–5. Or, streetcar No. 1 or No. 5 from Maidan (esplanade) passes theater, on your right just before Sree Arabinda Saranee (formerly Grey Street) crossing.

Theatre Centre, 31-A Chakraberia Road South. Phone 47–6175; English spoken. Hours: 6:30 P.M. weekends and irregular matinees. Prices variable. Hidden away off Sarat Bose Road. Take taxi, Rs3–5.

MADRAS

Kalakshetra Auditorium, Tiruvanmiyur, Adayar District. Phone 71–844; English spoken. Usually 6:15 P.M. Tickets Rs15, 10, 5 and (unreserved) 3. Can take special bus back to town, but only way there is by taxi: cross Adyar Bridge (just south of city) and turn left one-quarter mile at sign (in English) "Artists' Colony." Rs7–10.

Museum Theatre, Pantheon Road, Egmore District. Hours and prices variable. Taxi Rs3–5.

Music Academy Hall, corner Cathedral and Moybrays roads. Phone 81–2621; English spoken. Christmas festival hours: throughout the day and evening. Tickets Rs25, 15, 7, 3, 2. Taxi Rs3–5. Or, walk 300 yards to right from New Woodlands Hotel.

Mylapore Fine Arts Club, 10 Oliver Road, Mylapore District. Phone 72–660; English spoken. Hours: 6:30 P.M. Tickets Rs25, 15, 10, 5. Take taxi, Rs1–3.

N.K.T. Kalamantap, Peters Road, near Irusappa Gramani Street, Triplicane District. Hours, 6:30 P.M. Tickets Rs10, 7, 5, 3, 1. Take taxi, Rs2–4.

Rajah Annamalai Hall, 1 Esplanade, corner Esplanade and Fraser Bridge Road, near Fort Railway Station. Hours and prices variable. In north part of town, across the Cooum River. Take taxi, Rs3–5.

Rama Rau Kala Mantapa, Habibulla Road, T. Nagar District. Hours, 6:30 P.M. Tickets Rs15, 10, 5. Take taxi, Rs4–6.

Rasika Ranjani Sabha Hall, 2 Sundaraswarar Street, Mylapore District. Phone 71–767; English spoken. Hours 6:30 P.M. Tickets Rs10, 5, 3, 1. Taxi Rs3–5. Or, take city bus to Mylapore Bus Terminal, walk through Kapalleeswarar Temple to Sengaluneer Pillaiyer Koil Street, go right to first street, go left 100 yards; on left side of street.

South India Athletic Association, off Poonamallee High Road, Vepery District. Phone 27–788; English spoken. Hours 9:00–10:00 P.M. Park admission R1, theater admission, Rs5, 3, 2, 1. Taxi Rs3–5 to park entrance, then walk about 500 yards into park to far end.

Sri Krishna Gana Sabha, Govinda Street, T. Nagar District. Phone 44–2806, 44–1953; English spoken. Hours variable. Tickets Rs15, 10, 5, 2. Take taxi, Rs3–5. Theater is next to Ranagal Park.

University Centenary Auditorium, South Beach Road, Triplicane District. Phone sponsoring group. Hours and prices variable. Large, blocklike, white building set back from road. Taxi Rs3–5.

Vani Mahal, Gopathy Narayana Chetty Road, T. Nagar District. Hours variable. Tickets Rs15, 10, 5, 3. Take taxi, Rs4–6.

INDONESIA

djalan = street

DJAKARTA

Miss Tjitjih's, Djalan Salemba. Preliminary dances and songs, 8:00, and main play 8:45, P.M. First-class ticket 200 rupiah. In Kramat market area, one block from where Djalan Salemba becomes Djalan Kramat. Use taxi, helitjak, or betjak. Too far to walk from hotels.

Pantja Murti, Djalan Gunung Sari. Nightly at 8:00 P.M. First-class ticket 250 rupiah. Enter Djalan Gunung Sari (one way) off Banteng Square; theater is on your left just before reaching Pasar Senen market. Not far from Miss Tjitjih's. Take taxi, helitjak, or betjak. Too far to walk.

Ramayana Room, Hotel Indonesia, on Djalan Thamrin. Phone 41021, 43021, 46021; English spoken. Dinner and show 7–11 P.M. Normally Sunday; other nights occasionally. Hotel Indonesia is in the center of the city.

Taman Ismail Marzuki, 73 Djalan Tjikini Raya. Phone 42605; English spoken. Most days something is playing. Usually 8:00 P.M. Prices variable. Take taxi, helitjak, or betjak.

BALI

Konservatori Krawitan (KOKAR), Djalan Ratna, Den Pasar. Hours and prices vary. A short dokar ride from downtown Den Pasar; on the northern edge of the city, left side of the road toward Kesiman.

Lila Buana, corner Djalan Melati and Djalan Suratman, Den Pasar. Usually 7:30 P.M. Tickets 25 to 200 rupiah. On the bemo (panel truck) run between Den Pasar and Sanur: 10 rupiah from Den Pasar (catch bemo in front of Bali Hotel) or 25 rupiah from Sanur. Bemos are hard to find after midnight, so plan accordingly.

Radio Republic Indonesia Studio, 49 Djalan Melati, Den Pasar. A few blocks from Lila Buana. Usually 9:00 P.M. Tickets 100 rupiah or less. Can walk from downtown Den Pasar; or take taxi or dokar.

Teges Art Center, Teges Temple, Gianjar District. Inquire about dates, hours, and ticket prices. About 15 miles north of Den Pasar. Take taxi or bemo.

BANDUNG

Sri Murni, Djalan Jun Liong, Los 1–2, Pasar Kosambi. Nightly 8:00 P.M. First class 50 rupiah. Hard to find; facing Djalan Djenderal A Yani in front of Suryodadari theater, walk left to second narrow alley (Djalan Jun Liong), turn left up alley, pass Rivoli Movie, and theater is 100 feet ahead on your right.

Suryodadari, 77–79 Djalan Djenderal A Yani. Nightly 8:00 P.M. opening female dance; 8:30 P.M. play begins. First-class ticket 75 rupiah. Near Pasar Kosambi market and well-known; close to major hotels. By betjak about 75 rupiah. Up small pathway, about 50 feet off street.

JOGJAKARTA

Gedung Pertemuan Batik, Djalan Judonegaran. Usually 8:00 P.M. Tickets variable but not expensive. From North Palace Square (Alun-alun Lor), walk 100 feet up Djalan Judonegaran, the hall is on your left. Betjak 75 rupiah.

Loro Djonggrang Outdoor Theater, just off the main highway before entering Klaten from Jogjakarta. Hours 8:00 P.M. four nights a month. First-class ticket 3,000 rupiah or more. Hiring a taxi from Jogjakarta and having it wait is the easiest way; also special buses run from Jogjakarta; inquire at your hotel or travel agent.

Sosono Hinggil, Alun-alun Kidul (South Palace Square). Admission charge for Radio Republic Indonesia (RRI) broadcast performance 100 rupiah. Second Saturday of the month, 9:00 P.M. Take betjak 200 rupiah, or taxi 600 rupiah.

Taman Hiburan Rakjat, Djalan Gondomanan. Nightly at 8:30 P.M. First-class ticket 50–100 rupiah. Located at the rear of the city bus station. Betjak 150–200 rupiah.

SURAKARTA

Sri Wedari, Djalan Slamat Rijadi. Nightly 7:30 P.M. preliminary dances; 8:30 P.M. main play. First-class ticket 150 rupiah. Can easily walk: from Hotel Dana is just 100 yards to the right and across the street. Betjak or dokar 100 rupiah.

JAPAN

dori = street
michi = street

ku = city ward
cho = subward
chome = subsubward

TOKYO

Asakusa Engei Horu, 10, 2-chome, Asakusa, Taito-ku. On Sushiya

Yokochodori. Daily at 11:30 A.M. and 5:00 P.M. Tickets ¥800; buy at the door. To get there see **Kokusai Gekijo.**

Geijitsuza, 10–4, 1-chome, Yurakucho, Chiyoda-ku. Phone 591–1211; English spoken. Daily 5:30 P.M.; matinees Wednesday and Sunday 12:30 P.M. Tickets ¥3,000, 1,600. Taxi ¥300. Directly across the street from Takarazuka Gekijo. Box office on corner, theater entrance 50 feet along side facing the Imperial Hotel.

Haiyuza, 2–9–4 Roppongi, Minato-ku. Phone 403–2411; English sometimes spoken. Monday–Friday 6:30 P.M.; Saturday and Sunday 1:30 and 6:30 P.M. Tickets ¥1,800, 1,000. Taxi ¥500. Or, at Roppongi station of Hibiya Subway, go off platform in direction of Ginza, cross main Roppongi intersection to Mitsubishi Bank on corner; face bank, walk to your right 100 feet to next corner. A large sign (in English) "Actors' Theatre," identifies the theater on your left.

Honmokutei, 6–7, 2-chome, Ueno, Taito-ku. Phone 831–6137. Daily 12:00 noon and 6:00 P.M. Tickets ¥500 to ¥700. At Ueno Hirokoji station of Ginza Subway, go off platform in direction of Ueno, go straight ahead and upstairs to street level and continue about 100 feet, go left up second small alley, theater is on your left.

Jean-Jean, in Tokyo Yamate Church basement, 4 Udagawacho, Shibuya-ku. Phone 462–0641. Daily at 7:00 P.M.; also 1:00 P.M. matinees some days. Tickets ¥600–2,000, depending upon bill. Taxi ¥600–700. Or, from Shibuya train or subway station walk in direction of Shinjuku two blocks to Seibu Department Store, go left up rise 150 feet, church is modern concrete building on left.

Kabukiza, 3, 4-chome, Higashi Ginza, Chuo-ku. Phone 541–3131; English spoken. First 25 days of the month, 11:00–11:30 A.M. and 4:30–5:00 P.M. Tickets ¥4,000, 3,000, 2,000, 700. Taxi ¥350. Or, at Higashi Ginza station on Hibiya Subway take central exit and walk up steps immediately left of wicket. There are roman-letter signs "Kabukiza" on platform and passages. You come out directly in front of the theater.

Kanze Nogakudo, 1–16–4, Shoto, Shibuya-ku. Phone 469–5241. Regular Noh 10:30 A.M., first Sunday of the month. Tickets ¥3,000 reserved, ¥2,500 unreserved. Recommend taxi, ¥600. Not easy to find on foot, and a 30-minute walk, but: from Shibuya station walk to main Tokyu Department Store building several blocks away, go along the left side of the store to the back, cross the first small street and take the next street to your right about 500 yards up the rise and past the Swiss Embassy. Theater is at the end of the street, all stone, glass, and bronze.

Kinokuniya Horu, 4th floor, Kinokuniya Book Store, 12, 3-chome, Shinjuku-ku. Phone 354–0131. Hours variable. Tickets ¥1,800, 1,000. Taxi

¥600–700. Or, at Shinjuku Sanchome station of Marunouchi Subway, go off platform toward Shinjuku station, take exit No. 8 which leads straight to basement elevators in Kinokuniya Book Store. Play Guide is on the first floor; theater is on the fourth. Or from street level, Kinokuniya is the unmistakable narrow, olive-brown ceramic brick building on Shinjukudori across the street from Mitsukoshi Department Store.

Kokuritsu Gekijo, 13, Hayabusacho, Chiyoda-ku. Phone 265–7411; English spoken. Hours vary with type of performance, but normally 11:30 A.M. and/or 4:30–5:00 P.M. Tickets ¥2,500, 2,000, 1,500, 700 in large theater and ¥1,800, 1,200 in small theater. Difficult to walk to. Recommend taxi, ¥400.

Kokusai Gekijo, 17, 3-chome, Nishi Asakusa, Taito-ku. Phone 844–1144; English spoken. Daily 2:30 and 6:30 P.M. Tickets ¥2,300, 1,800, 1,400, 1,100. Taxi ¥1,000. Suggest go by subway. Take Ginza Subway (not Tozai Subway) to Asakusa station, exit to front of train going straight through wicket and up inclined passage 50 feet, turn sharp left and go up steps to street, take the street crossing which bears slightly right, walk 30 feet to major intersection, right 200 feet on Asakusadori to the Red Gate (Kaminarimon) on your right that leads to Kannon Temple. At temple go left, keeping little park with fountain on your right and multitowered pagoda on your left. In two blocks you will reach Kokusaidori, after passing a small tea house, Mokubakan theater, Asakusa Engei Horu, and the famous cross street which is filled with a score of triple-feature movie houses, strip joints, massage parlors, and the like. Turn right, go one block on Kokusaidori, and the theater is across the street on your left. Look for large sign "Kokusai Theatre."

Meijiza, 1–30, 2-chome, Nihonbashi, Chuo-ku. Phone 677–5151. First 25 days of the month 11:30 A.M. and 4:30–5:00 P.M. Tickets ¥3,200, 2,500, 1,200, 600. Taxi ¥600. Or, at Ningyocho station on Hibiya Subway, exit in direction of Kayabacho taking exit on left after wicket; at street level go left 10 feet to corner, turn left and walk five blocks to major intersection; theater is across street on your left.

Mokubakan, Mokubakandori, 2-chome, Asakusa, Taito-ku. Daily from 11:00 A.M. to 9:00 P.M. All seats unreserved, ¥800. To get there see **Kokusai Geikijo.**

Nakano Umewaka Gakuin Kaikan, 6–14, Higashi Nakano, 2-chome, Nakano-ku. Phone 363–7749; English spoken. Regular Noh each third Sunday, 11:00 A.M. or 12:00 noon. Tickets ¥3,000–4,000. Taxi ¥1,000. Or, take yellow train of the Boso surface line (Chuo line) to Higashi Nakano, go off the platform in the direction of Nakano station; keeping left, walk forward 200 feet along train tracks to bridge, turn left and walk on main road (Yamatedori, but unmarked) about 600 yards (down hill past bowling alley and shrine torii); by Higashi Nakano 2-chome bus stop (look for round sign on post, no roman letters) where street curves to left, a wide opening on the right side of the street leads to theater, which is set back from the road.

Nichigeki Mujiku Horu, 1, 2-chome, Yurakucho, Chiyoda-ku. Phone 201–0050; English spoken. Hours have not changed for the past twenty years: weekdays 2:30, 4:50, and 7:10 P.M.; Saturday and Sunday, 12:30, 2:50, 5:10, and 7:30 P.M. Reserved seats ¥1,700, unreserved seats ¥1,200. Taxi ¥200. Or, facing Nihon Gekijo (see below) go around to entrance marked "Nichigeki Music Hall" on left side of building, buy ticket, then take elevator to fifth floor.

Nihon Gekijo, 1, 2-chome, Yurakucho, Chiyoda-ku. Phone 201–2111; English spoken. Daily at 1:00 and 5:30 P.M. Tickets ¥2,200, 1,900, 1,000. Taxi ¥250. Or at Ginza station of Marunouchi Subway, go out wicket toward Kasumigaseki, take exit No. 20 on your right; at top of steps you will see distinctive curving front of the theater directly across the street.

Nissei Gekijo, 14, 1-chome, Yurakucho, Chiyoda-ku. Phone 591–1211; English spoken. Hours vary. Tickets about ¥3,500, 2,800, 1,500, and 800. Taxi ¥300. The theater is at the back of Takarazuka Gekijo, opposite the new wing of the Imperial Hotel.

Shimbashi Embujo, 2–18, 6-chome, Ginza, Chuo-ku. Phone 541–2211. Daily 11:00 A.M. and 4:30–5:00 P.M. Tickets ¥3,500, 2,500, 1,800, and 800. Taxi ¥400. Or, at Higashi Ginza station of Hibiya Subway, exit at end of platform toward Tsukiji, take first exit to right after wicket, walk right two blocks (past Ginza Tokyu Hotel); theater is on your left.

Shinjuku Bunka, 21, 2-chome, Shinjuku-ku. Phone 351–3414. One performance nightly at 9:30 P.M. Tickets ¥1,000. Taxi ¥700–800. Or, at Shinjuku Sanchome station of Marunouchi Subway, go off platform in direction of Shinjuku Gyoenmae, take exit No. 1; at street level turn right on Meijidori and walk 200 yards (opposite Isetan Department Store); it is the second movie house on your right.

Shinjuku Koma Gekijo, 19, Kabukicho, Shinjuku-ku. Phone 202–0131; English spoken. Daily 11:00–11:30 A.M. and 4:30 P.M. Tickets ¥1,800, 1,500, 1,000, and 600. Taxi ¥700–800. Or, at Shinjuku station of Marunouchi Subway go off platform in direction of Shinjuku Sanchome, go left after wicket and take exit No. 16 to street level, keeping to the left up the stairs, turn right and go 20 feet to first street, turn right and continue across broad avenue (Yasukunidori) and another 200 feet ahead to dead end. Theater is to your right with (English) sign "Koma Stadium."

Shinohara Engeijo, near Jujo station, Kita-ku. Nightly at 6:30 P.M. Admission ¥200 plus ¥10 to rent a cushion. This is a bit far out: at Jujo station, two stops out from Ikebukuro on the Akabane surface line, go out the left exit at the forward end of the station, turn right and follow the tracks, turn right at first narrow street, cross tracks, and go straight about 200 yards through bustling market; theater is on your left.

Suehirotei, 2-chome, Suehirodori, Shinjuku-ku. Daily at 12:00 noon and 5:00 P.M. All tickets ¥700. Taxi ¥700–800. Or at Shinjuku Sanchome station of Marunouchi Subway, exit in direction of Shinjuku Gyoenmae, go out exit No. 1; at street level turn right 180 degrees and go down small street 100 feet to second alleyway, turn left, go 50 feet; theater with red and white lanterns as a marquee is on your left.

Suidobashi Nohgakudo, 5–9, 1-chome, Hongo, Bunkyo-ku. Phone 811–4843; English spoken. Hours and prices variable. Taxi ¥600–700. Or, take yellow train of Boso surface line (Chuo line) to Suidobashi station, and leave platform in direction of Ochanomizu, go left across bridge over canal and straight through major intersection, cross over to the right side of the street and at the first side street turn right one short block. Theater is low, tile-brick building on the corner.

Suzumoto Engeijo, Chuodori, 2-chome, Ueno, Taito-ku. Phone 832–0874. Daily 1:00 and 3:30 P.M. Tickets around ¥800, depending on bill. To get there, see **Honmokutei**. Instead of turning left up alley, go straight ahead another 60 feet; theater is in new, grey-brick office building on your left. Buy ticket at door and take escalator to second floor theater.

Takarazuka Gekijo, 10–2, 1-chome, Yurakucho, Chiyoda-ku. Phone 591–1211; English spoken. One performance daily 5:30 P.M., except Saturday, 2:30 and 5:30 P.M., and Sunday, 11:00 A.M. and 4:00 P.M. Tickets ¥2,800, 1,800, 800, and 400. This is a very easy theater to find; it is across the street from the Imperial Hotel at the end of block-long "Toho Amusement Street" (Toho Yurakugai). If you are coming by subway, get out at Hibiya station of Hibiya Subway line, go out exit in direction of Ginza, follow signs in subway to Imperial Hotel.

Teikoku Gekijo, 12, 3-chome, Marunouchi, Chiyoda-ku. Phone 213–7311, English spoken. Hours variable. Tickets ¥3,000, 2,400, 1,000, and 500. Taxi ¥300. Or, at Hibiya station of Hibiya Subway line, leave the platform in direction of Kasumigaseki, turn sharply left after wicket, climb stairs and take second exit on your right to the street. Theater occupies whole second block on your right and faces Imperial Palace moat.

Tenjo Sajikikan, 22, Higashicho, Shibuya-ku. Phone 409–1157. Usually at 8:00 P.M., except Sunday. Tickets ¥900, 800, or lower. Taxi ¥700–800. Or, from in front of Tokyo Bunka Kaikan Building and facing Shibuya station, go left, take overpass across Tamagawadori, descend in front of Shibuya Police Station and continue going straight on Meijidori three short blocks. The theater is on the left (by a gasoline station) with its psychedelic front impossible to miss.

Theatro Echo, 18–18, 1-chome, Ebisu, Shibuya-ku. Phone 44–5058.

Hours variable. Tickets ¥1,500 and worth it. Theater is not easy to find. Taxi ¥700. Or, at Ebisu station on Yamate surface line, walk on platform in direction of Meguro, take bridge over tracks, go down steep steps in front of station and go straight one block, across wide street, and 300 yards farther. Theater is on your left.

Toho Engeijo, 5th floor, Takarazuka Building, 12, 1-chome, Yurakucho, Chiyoda-ku. Weekdays 6:00 P.M.; Saturday, Sunday, and holidays 1:30 and 6:00 P.M. Reserved tickets ¥850, unreserved tickets ¥650. Buy at ground-level box office. For directions see **Takarazuka Gekijo**.

Toyoko Gekijo, 9th floor, Toyoko branch, Tokyu Department Store, Shibuya station building. Phone 462–4271. Hours and prices variable. First class goes back 26 rows. Taxi ¥700. There are no signs to help, but go to the main lobby of Shibuya station building and take elevator from ground level in west wing (next to escalators) to ninth floor.

Yarai Nogakudo, 60 Yaraicho, Shinjuku-ku. Phone 268–7311. Hours and prices variable. Taxi ¥600. Or, coming from downtown on the Tozai Subway get off at Kagurazaka station, go out exit at front of train, cross the street and go about 200 yards (up rising street that is the shank of the "T" crossing), at first street to the right turn and go about 30 feet. Theater is on your right set back from the street.

KYOTO

Gion Corner, 1st floor of Yasaka Hall, Hanamikojidori, Gion, Higashi-yama-ku. Phone 561–1115; English spoken. Twice daily, 8:00 and 9:10 P.M., March 1 to November 29. Tickets ¥1,500. Be sure to walk: from Shijo Bridge go past Minamiza on Shijodori two short blocks, turn right on Hanamikoji-dori, go 200 yards (past excellent Junidanya steak house); theater is through large entryway on your left.

Gion Kaburenjo, Nanamikojidori, Gion, Higashiyama-ku. Phone 561–1117. Hours variable. Tickets about ¥2,000. Theater adjoins Yasaka Hall; for directions see **Gion Corner**.

Kongo Nogakudo, Muromachidori off Shijodori, Nakagyo-ku. Phone 221–3049. Hours and prices variable. Taxi ¥300–500. Or, at corner of Shijodori and Kasumadori, walk one block west (away from Gion, past Sanwa Bank), turn right and go 200 feet; wooden entryway with tile half-roof leads to theater set back from street. There are no signs in roman letters.

Kyoto Furitsu Bunka Geijitsu Kaikan Horu, corner Kawaramachi and Hirokojidori, Shinomiyako-ku. Phone 222–0847. Hours variable. Tickets ¥800 or less. Taxi ¥400–500. Or take streetcar north on Kawarama-chidori and get off at Furitsu Byoin Mae stop; step out of car into theater entrance.

Kyoto Kaikan, Saishojimachi, Okazaki, Sagyo-ku. Phone 771–6051. Hours and prices variable. Taxi ¥400–500. Or, standing on street before entrance to Heian Shrine, face the great gate (torii) over Jingumichi, walk toward the torii one block, turn right and go half a block; it is the huge modern structure on your right. The small theater is on your left as you go in, and the large theater straight ahead. Or take streetcar No. 22 from downtown to Okazaki Koen Mae stop, walk to your right two blocks, theaters are on your left.

Kyoto Kanze Kaikan, 44, Ensojimachi, Okazaki, Sagyo-ku. Phone 771–6114. Irregular hours. Tickets ¥2,000 or less. Taxi ¥400. Or, standing before entrance to Heian Shrine, face the great gate (torii) over Jingumichi, walk two blocks (through the gate and across a canal), walk right about 100 feet; the theater is on your left.

Minamiza, Higashigawa, Shijo Ohashi, Higashiyama-ku. Phone 561–1155. Twice daily, at 11:30 A.M. and 4:30–5:00 P.M. Tickets ¥2,400 to ¥400. Taxi ¥300. Or, standing in middle of Shijo Bridge and facing the Shijo station of Keishin surface line, the theater is in view on your right.

Oe Nogakudo, Yanagibanba, Oshikoji, Nakagyo-ku. Phone 231–7625. Hours and prices variable. Taxi ¥400–500. Or, get off streetcar No. 5 (coming from downtown) at Karasuma Oike stop, turn right and go six short blocks on Oikedori, go left one block on Yanaginobanbadori, then right 75 feet; look for sign under archway in roman letters "Oe Nogakudo" on your right.

Pontocho Kaburenjo, Sanjo Ohashi-han, Nakagyo-ku. Phone 221–2025. Three performances daily in season. Tickets about ¥1,000. Taxi ¥300–400. Or, walk to the end of Pontocho Lane by Sanjo Bridge; theater is on your right.

NAGOYA

Chunichi Gekijo, 9th floor Chunichi Newspaper Building, 1–1, 4-chome, Sakae, Naka-ku. Phone 261–2045. Hours variable. Tickets ¥2,800–1,000 top. Taxi ¥300. On corner Hisayadori and Hirokojidori; look for English sign "Tokai Bank" and go in right side entrance to elevators. Or, take subway from Nagoya station, get off at Sakae station (second stop), go out middle exit, turning right after wicket, go down short flight of stairs and straight to end of underground store corridor (100 yards), turn left, jog right, and on your left are elevators that will take you to the 9th floor.

Meitetsu Horu, 10th floor, Meitetsu Department Store Building, 223–1 Sasajimacho, Nakamura-ku. Phone 561–4916. Hours vary; sometimes matinee. Tickets ¥3,000, 2,000, 1,000, 300. Theater is 100 yards from Nagoya station, Meitetsu Department Store is first building on your right. Go in side entrance toward rear of building and take elevator to 10th floor.

Misonoza, 14–6, 1-chome, Sakae, Naka-ku. Phone 211–1451. Daily 11:00 A.M. and 4:00 P.M. Tickets ¥3,000 to ¥600. Taxi ¥300–400. Or, take subway from Nagoya station to Fushimi station (first stop), cross under tracks to go out exit No. 4, keeping on right side of Fushimidori, cross Hikojidori, and turn right at second small sidestreet; entrance to theater is on your right.

OSAKA

Asahiza, 1 Higashi Yaguracho, Minami-ku. Phone 211–6431. Matinee 12:00 noon and evening 5:00 or 6:30 P.M. Tickets ¥2,800 and less, depending on bill. Taxi ¥500–600. Or, at Namba station on Midosuji Subway go off platform in direction of Umeda station, go straight through wicket to end of underground passage (about 100 yards), go out right exit, at street level continue in same direction as underground passage (i.e.: turn 180 degrees at top of stairs) 100 feet to Dotombori and turn right just before the river. Or, facing the street in front of Shin Kabukiza turn left and walk about 250 yards along Midosujidori to Dotombori River, and turn right.

Festibaru Horu, 3rd floor, Shin Asahi Biru, 22, 2-chome Nakanoshima, Kita-ku. Phone 231–2222. Hours variable. Tickets up to ¥6,000. Taxi ¥400. Can enter first floor of Shin Asahi Biru from rear of Hotel Osaka Grand, then take escalator to lobby on second floor. Or at Yodoyabashi station of Midosuji Subway, go off platform in direction of Umeda, taking exit on your left immediately after wicket, walk toward and across bridge, continue one block and turn left on Nakanoshimadori, go about 600 yards to next bridge and intersection with Yotsubashisujidori, to the shiny aluminum building on your left.

Kadoza, Nishi Yaguracho, Minami-ku. Phone 211–0277. Daylong program from 11:30 A.M. Tickets ¥800. Taxi ¥500–600. See **Asahiza** for directions.

Nakaza, Nishi Yaguracho, Minami-ku. Phone 211–1567. Daily 11:30 A.M. and 4:30 P.M. Tickets ¥2,700, 2,000, and 1,000. Taxi ¥500–600. See **Asahiza** for directions.

Shin Kabukiza, 5–59, Namba Shinchi, Minami-ku. On Midosujidori a few blocks from Dotombori. Phone 631–2121. Hours variable. Tickets ¥3,300, 2,400, 1,800, 1,200, 800. Taxi ¥500–600. Or, at Namba station of Midosuji Subway, go out in direction away from Umeda, taking right exit after wicket. Theater is 50 feet straight ahead and opposite Takashimaya Department Store.

Takarazuka Dai Gekijo, Takarazuka City, about 20 miles from Osaka. Daily 1:00 or 3:00 P.M. and Sunday 10:30 A.M. matinee. Tickets ¥1,000, 700,

500, and 300 (plus ¥300 for admission to Takarazuka Park). To get there, take Hankyu air-conditioned express train from Umeda station in Osaka to end of line (40 minutes, ¥90). Or from Kobe, take Osaka-bound Hankyu express train from Sannomiya station and change to Takarazuka line at Nishinomiya Kitaguchi station. Follow the stream of girls from the station two blocks to Takarazuka Park entrance. The main theater is to your left inside the gate and the smaller theater is on your right.

Umeda Koma Gekijo, 5-Kakudàcho, Kita-ku. Phone 313–3251. Hours variable. Tickets ¥2,000, 1,600, 750, and 600. Taxi ¥300–400. Or, from the maze of passageways beneath Umeda station go off platform of Midosuji Subway in direction of New Osaka station; turn right after wicket and go straight 300 yards to dead end, take exit, turn left, and the theater is to your right under the railroad tracks. It's hardly worth it.

KOREA

ku = city ward
dong = subward
ro = avenue
ka = side street

SEOUL

Cafe Theatre, 24–11, 1-ka Choongmoo-ro. Phone 23–3525; English spoken. Irregular nights of the week at 8:00 P.M. Tickets won 400. Taxi probably won't know, so get off at Savoy Hotel on Choongmoo-ro (won 200–300); facing street, walk right 100 yards, cross street and go to end of small alley just right of Korea Exchange Bank.

Drama Centre of Korea, 8 Yejang-dong, Joong-ku, Namsan. Phone 23–3410, 22–7661; English spoken. Hours and tickets variable. Taxi won 200–300.

Korea House, 82, 2-ka Pil-dong, Choong-ku. Phone 22–0752, 23–6749; English spoken. Always 3:00 P.M. Free. Taxi won 250–300. Or, facing street in front of Sejong Hotel (Toege-ro), walk left to Y-shaped intersection (about 600 yards), bear right 150 feet and enter large traditional Korean archway.

Kulip Kukjang (National Theater), 2-ka Chang Choong-dong. Hours and prices variable. Take taxi, won 300–400. Too far to walk. Next to Chang Choong-dong Park. Entrance is opposite entrance to Tower Hotel.

Yesul Kukjang (Old National Theater), 1-ka Myong-dong. Usually 3:30 P.M. matinee and 7:30 P.M. evening performance. Tickets variable. Taxi won 100–200. Or, standing in front of the UNESCO building, theater is across the street on your right.

MALAYSIA

jalan = road
leboh = street

KUALA LUMPUR

Dewan Bandaran, corner Jalan Tuanku Abdul Rahman and Jalan Mountbatten. Phone 25471; English spoken. Hours and prices variable. From Robinson's department store on Jalan Mountbatten go right to intersection with Jalan Tuanku Abdul Rahman; building is on your left, entrance 300 yards to far side of building by river.

Panggong Anniversary, Jalan Tembusu in Lake Gardens. Hours variable. Usually free. Take taxi, M$4–6.

Panggong Derama, in Majlis Derama Malaysia Building, on Jalan Bandar across from Central Police Station. Hours and prices variable. Take taxi, M$2–4.

Panggong Eksperimen, University of Malaysia campus, south edge of city. Hours and prices variable. Taxi M$6–8. In same building with Dewan Tunku Chancellor fieldhouse.

PENANG

Dewan Sri Pinang, corner of Leboh Light and Leboh Pitt, across from the Supreme Court. Phone 24700 and 62340. Hours and prices variable. A 10-minute walk from the E. and O. Hotel: follow Leboh Farquhar to Leboh Pitt, turn left to Leboh Light. Or M$1 by trishaw.

Sasaran, on Universiti Sains Malaysia campus, four miles south of Georgetown. Phone 25311. ext. 371. Usually 8:00 P.M.; tickets M$2. Take taxi M$4–5 or Blue Bus marked Bayan Lepas from Jalan Maxwell Station in Georgetown (M20¢) to Universiti stop, walk 15 minutes up hill to main campus area, bear left and descend to rear of campus.

PHILIPPINES

MANILA

Cultural Center of the Philippines (CCP), Roxas Boulevard opposite Vito Cruz Avenue. Hours and prices vary with the program. CCP is about 40 minutes walk from major hotels and the American Embassy along the beautifully landscaped harbor front. For the **Main Theater** go up the great curving ramp leading to the front entrance of the CCP; the **Little Theater** entrance is around the building on the right side; the **Folk Art Theater** is behind main CCP theater. Taxi ₱3–4.

Open Air Auditorium, opposite the large fountain on the north side of

Luneta (Rizal) National Park, next to American Embassy. Hours vary with program; about 7:30 P.M. May be free or small charge for admission. A 2-block walk from Manila Hilton.

Philamlife Auditorium, United Nations Avenue at Maria Y. Orosa Avenue. Hours and prices variable. A one-block walk from Manila Hilton.

Rajah Sulaiman Theatre-in-Ruins, Fort Santiago, Intramuros. Hours and prices depend upon the program. Going north on Bonifacio Drive from the Luneta, turn right on Aduana Ave. to Manila Cathedral, enter Fort Santiago opposite the cathedral; it is on your right near the river. Taxi ₱3–4.

SINGAPORE

Cultural Centre Theatre, Canning Rise 6. Phone 360005; English spoken. Hours vary, inquire. Ticket prices usually S$3, 2, 1. Taxi S$1–3. A bit tricky to find walking because it doesn't look like a theater. Is downstairs in white concrete building marked "Adult Education Board," directly behind and visible from National Museum, but is not accessible from there. About a 10-minute walk from Adelphi Hotel: walk left up Coleman Street toward hill and continue up hill where it connects with Canning Rise.

National Theatre, Clemenceau Avenue 9. Phone 22058; English spoken. Hours and prices vary. Taxi S$1–3. Or, about a 15-minute walk from Victoria Theatre, straight up River Valley Road; theater is on your right just past Van Kleef Aquarium.

Singapore Conference Hall, Shenton Way 1. Phone 97671; English spoken. Usually 8:00 or 8:30 P.M. Prices vary. Taxi S$3–4. At Shenton Circus, near the South Wharf. Too far to walk comfortably.

Victoria Theatre, Empress Place 6, just next to Singapore Cricket Club. Phone 27490 or 362151; English spoken. Usually 8:30 P.M. Prices vary. Taxi S$1–3. Or, 15- to 20-minute walk south on Beach Road, continuing into Connaught Drive, which ends at Empress Place.

Wisma Theatre, 435 Orchard Road 9, opposite C. K. Tang Department Store. Phone 363422. Often as early as 7:30 P.M. Tickets S$5, 4, 3. Taxi S$1–2. Or, an easy walk from Orchard Road hotels. Enter far left end of Wisma Indonesia building facade; can't see theater from the street.

THAILAND

BANGKOK

Culture Hall, on Raj Damnoen Avenue near Sri Ayuthya Road. Hours and prices variable. Taxi bhat 15–20. Look for the large building set back from the road.

Lok Muang, Sanam Chai Road, near Royal Palace. Daily 9:00 A.M. until

3:00 P.M. No admission, but you can, if you wish, drop a few coins in the temple offertory box. Taxi bhat 10–12. Or, from Silpakorn Theater walk kitty-corner all the way across Pra Mane Ground. The temple, a small building, is outside the ground, across Sanam Chai Road, tucked in behind the gasoline station on the corner.

Sangkhit Sala, river side of Pra Mane Ground. Weekends only, matinee around 4:00 P.M. Ticket bhat 3. Taxi bhat 10–15. Enter through National Museum gates. There is no sign indicating the theater.

Silpakorn, river side of Pra Mane Ground. Hours and prices variable. Taxi bhat 10–15. Theater is immediately to the right of the National Museum, on the corner.

VIETNAM

SAIGON

Olympic, Hung Thap Tu Street. Wednesday through Sunday, 8:00 P.M. Tickets 500–800 piasters. Take taxi, 200–400 piasters.

Quoc Thanh, Vo Tanh Street. Wednesday through Sunday, 8:00 P.M. Tickets 600–800 piasters. Taxi 300–450 piasters.